THE HYMN BOOK

ISBN 978-0-634-01234-1

HAL•LEONARD®
CORPORATION
7777 W. BLUEMOUND RD. P.O. BOX 13819 MILWAUKEE, WI 53213

Visit Hal Leonard Online at
www.halleonard.com

THE HYMN BOOK

STRUM AND PICK PATTERNS

This chart contains the suggested strum and pick patterns that are referred to by number at the beginning of each song in this book. The symbols ⊓ and ∨ in the strum patterns refer to down and up strokes, respectively. The letters in the pick patterns indicate which right-hand fingers plays which strings.

p = **thumb**
i = **index finger**
m = **middle finger**
a = **ring finger**

For example; Pick Pattern 2
is played: thumb - index - middle - ring

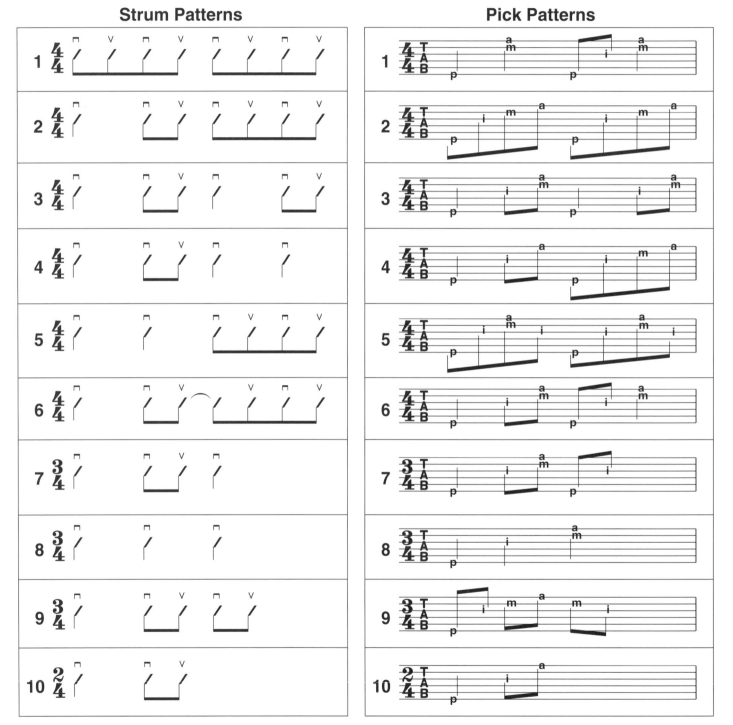

Strum Patterns   **Pick Patterns**

You can use the 3/4 Strum or Pick Patterns in songs written in compound meter (6/8, 9/8, 12/8, etc.).
For example, you can accompany a song in 6/8 by playing the 3/4 pattern twice in each measure.
The 4/4 Strum and Pick Patterns can be used for songs written in cut time (¢) by doubling the note time values in the patterns. Each pattern would therefore last two measures in cut time.

All Creatures of Our God and King

Words by Francis of Assisi
Music from *Geistliche Kirchengesäng*

*Strum Pattern: 4 & 10
*Pick Pattern: 4 & 10

*Combine patterns

Additional Lyrics

2. Thou rushing wind that art so strong,
   Ye clouds that sail in heav'n along,
   Oh praise Him, alleluia!
   Thou rising morn in praise rejoice,
   Ye lights of evening, find a voice,

3. Thou flowing water, pure and clear,
   Make music for thy Lord to hear,
   Oh praise Him, alleluia!
   Thou fire so masterful and bright,
   Thou givest man both warmth and light,

4. And all ye men of tender heart,
   Forgiving others, take your part,
   Oh sing ye, alleluia!
   Ye who long pain and sorrow bear,
   Praise God and on Him cast your care,

5. Let all things their Creator bless,
   And worship Him in humbleness,
   Oh praise Him, alleluia!
   Praise, praise the Father, praise the Son,
   And praise the Spirit, three in one,

Abide With Me

Words by Henry F. Lyte
Music by W.H. Monk

Strum Pattern: 4
Pick Pattern: 5

Verse
Moderately

1. A - bide with me; fast falls the e - ven tide. The dark - ness deep - ens;
2., 3., 4. *See Additional Lyrics*

Lord, with me a - bide! When oth - er help - ers fail and com - forts flee,

help of the help - less, oh, a - bide with me. me.

Additional Lyrics

2. Swift to its close ebbs out life's little day.
Earth's joys grow dim, its glories pass away.
Change and decay in all around I see.
Oh, Thou who changest not, abide with me.

3. I need Thy presence every passing hour;
What but Thy grace can foil the tempter's power?
Who like Thy self, my guide and stay can be?
Through cloud and sunshine, Lord, abide with me.

4. I fear no foe with Thee at hand to bless.
Ills have no weight, and tears no bitterness.
Where is death's sting? Where, grave, thy victory?
I triumph still if Thou abide with me.

Alas, and Did My Savior Bleed

Words by Isaac Watts
Music by Hugh Wilson

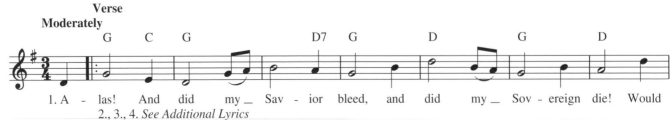

Strum Pattern: 8
Pick Pattern: 8

Verse
Moderately

1. A - las! And did my _ Sav - ior bleed, and did my _ Sov - ereign die! Would
2., 3., 4. *See Additional Lyrics*

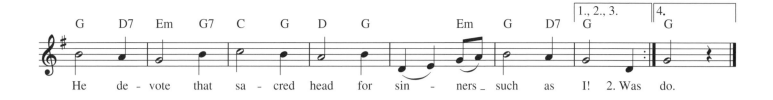

He de- vote that sa- cred head for sin- ners_ such as I! 2. Was do.

Additional Lyrics

2. Was it for sins that I have done
   He suffered on the tree?
   Amazing pity! Grace unknown!
   And love beyond degree!

3. Well might the sun in darkness hide,
   And shut its glories in,
   When Christ, the great Redeemer, died
   For human creatures' sin.

4. But drops of grief can ne'er repay
   The debt of love I owe;
   Here, Lord, I give myself away;
   'Tis all that I can do.

All Hail the Power of Jesus' Name

Words by Edward Perronet
Music by William Shrubsole

Strum Pattern: 4
Pick Pattern: 4

Verse
Moderately

1. All hail the pow'r of Je- sus' name. Let an- gels pros- trate
2., 3. *See Additional Lyrics*

fall. Bring forth the roy- al di- a- dem and crown Him

Lord of _____ all. Bring forth the roy- al di- a- dem and

crown Him Lord _____ of all. 2. Let all.

Additional Lyrics

2. Let ev'ry kindred, ev'ry tribe on this terrestrial ball.
   To Him all majesty ascribe and crown Him Lord of all.
   To Him all majesty ascribe and crown Him Lord of all.

3. Oh, that with yonder sacred throng we at His feet may fall.
   We'll join the everlasting song and crown Him Lord of all.
   We'll join the everlasting song and crown Him Lord of all.

All the Way My Savior Leads Me

Words by Fanny J. Crosby
Music by Robert Lowry

C G F D G7

Strum Pattern: 9
Pick Pattern: 7

Verse
Moderately Slow

1. All the way my Sav - ior leads me; what have I to ask be -
2., 3. *See Additional Lyrics*

side? Can I doubt His ten - der mer - cy, who through life has been my guide? Heav'n - ly

peace, di - vin - est com - fort, here by faith in Him to dwell! For I

know what e'er be - fall me, Je - sus do - eth all things well; for I

know what-e'er be - fall me, Je - sus do - eth all things well. 2. All the way.

Additional Lyrics

2. All the way my Savior leads me; cheers each winding path I tread,
Gives me grace for ev'ry trial, feeds me with the living bread.
Though my weary steps may falter, and my soul athirst may be,
Gushing from the rock before me, Lo! A spring of joy I see;
Gushing from the rock before me, Lo! A spring of joy I see.

3. All the way my Savior leads me; O the fulness of His love!
Perfect rest to me is promised in my Father's house above.
When my spirit, clothed immortal, wings its flight to realms of day,
This my song through endless ages: Jesus led me all the way;
This my song through endless ages: Jesus led me all the way.

All Things Bright and Beautiful

Words by Cecil Frances Alexander
17th Century English Melody
Arranged by Martin Shaw

Strum Pattern: 4
Pick Pattern: 4

Additional Lyrics

2. The purple headed mountains, the river running by,
   The sunset and the morning that brightens up the sky.

3. The cold wind in the winter, the pleasant summer sun,
   The ripe fruits in the garden; God made them everyone.

4. God gave us eyes to see them, and lips that we might tell
   How great is God almighty, who has made all things well.

All Your Anxiety

Traditional

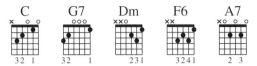

Strum Pattern: 8
Pick Pattern: 8

Additional Lyrics

2. No other friend so swift to help you;
   No other friend so quick to hear.
   No other place to leave your burden;
   No other one to hear your prayer.

3. Come then at once; delay no longer!
   Heed His entreaty kind and sweet.
   You need not fear a disappointment;
   You shall find peace at the mercy seat.

Amazing Grace

Words by John Newton
Traditional American Melody

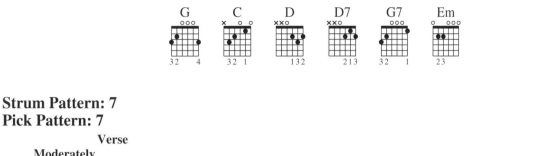

Strum Pattern: 7
Pick Pattern: 7

Verse
Moderately

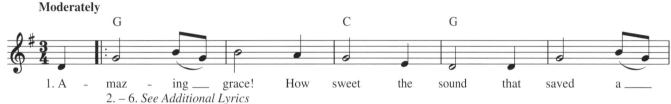

1. A - maz - ing __ grace! How sweet the sound that saved a __
2. – 6. *See Additional Lyrics*

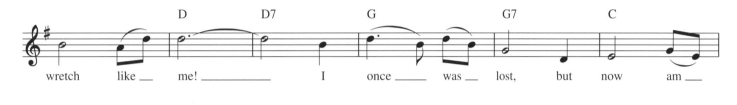

wretch like __ me! __ I once __ was __ lost, but now am __

found, was blind, but __ now I see. __ 2. 'Twas __

Additional Lyrics

2. 'Twas grace that taught my heart to fear,
   And grace my fears relieved.
   How precious did that grace appear
   The hour I first believed.

3. Through many dangers, toils and snares,
   I have already come.
   'Tis grace has brought me safe thus far,
   And grace will lead me home.

4. The Lord has promised good to me,
   His word my hope secures.
   He will my shield and portion be
   As long as life endures.

5. And when this flesh and heart shall fail,
   And mortal life shall cease.
   I shall posess within the veil
   A life of joy and peace.

6. When we've been there ten thousand years,
   Bright shining as the sun.
   We've no less days to sing God's praise
   Than when we first begun.

And Can It Be That I Should Gain

Words by Charles Wesley
Music by Thomas Campbell

Strum Pattern: 1, 3
Pick Pattern: 2, 4

Additional Lyrics

2. He left His Father's throne above;
So free, so infinite His grace.
Emptied Himself of all but love,
And bled for Adam's helpless race.
'Tis mercy all, immense and free,
For, O my God, it found out me.

3. Long my imprisoned spirit lay
Fast bound in sin and nature's night;
Thine eye diffused a quick'ning ray,
I woke, the dungeon flamed with light.
My chains fell off; my heart was free.
I rose, went forth and followed Thee.

4. No condemnation now I dread;
Jesus, and all in Him is mine!
Alive in Him, my living head,
And clothed in righteousness divine;
Bold I approach th'eternal throne
And claim the crown, thro' Christ, my own.

At Calvary

Words by William Newell
Music by D.B. Towner

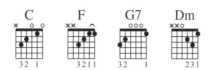

Strum Pattern: 4
Pick Pattern: 2, 4

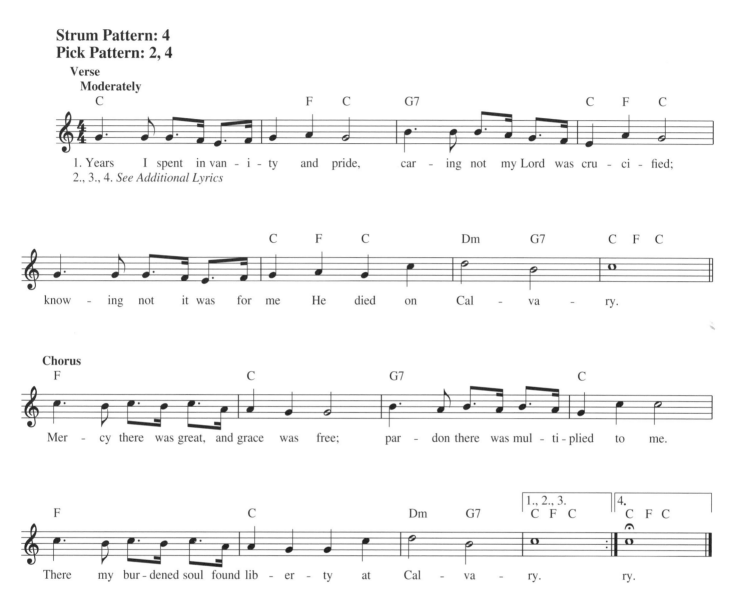

1. Years I spent in van - i - ty and pride, car - ing not my Lord was cru - ci - fied;
2., 3., 4. *See Additional Lyrics*

know - ing not it was for me He died on Cal - va - ry.

Chorus

Mer - cy there was great, and grace was free; par - don there was mul - ti - plied to me.

There my bur - dened soul found lib - er - ty at Cal - va - ry. ry.

Additional Lyrics

2. By God's Word at last my sin I learned;
   Then I trembled at the law I'd spurned,
   Till my guilty soul imploring turned to Calvary.

3. Now I've giv'n to Jesus ev'rything,
   Now I gladly own Him as my King,
   Now my raptured soul can only sing of Calvary.

4. Oh, the love that drew salvation's plan!
   Oh, the grace that brought it down to man!
   Oh, the mighty gulf that God did span at Calvary.

At the Cross

Text by Isaac Watts
Music by Ralph E. Hudson

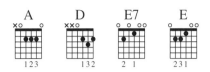

Strum Pattern: 2
Pick Pattern: 4

Additional Lyrics

2. Was it for crimes that I have done He groaned upon the tree?
   Amazing pity! Grace unknown! And love beyond degree!

3. Well might the sun in darkness hole and shut His glories in,
   When Christ, the mighty Maker, died for man the creature's sin.

4. But drops of grief can ne'er repay the debt of love I owe:
   Here, Lord, I give myself away; 'tis all that I can do!

Be Still My Soul

Words by Katharina von Schegel
Music by Jean Sibelius

Strum Pattern: 4
Pick Pattern: 1

Additional Lyrics

2. Be still, my soul, thy God doth undertake
To guide the future as He has the past.
Thy hope, thy confidence let nothing shake.
All now mysterious shall be bright at last.
Be still, my soul; the wave and wind still know
His voice who ruled them while He dwelt below.

3. Be still, my soul; the hour is hast'ning on
When we shall be forever with the Lord,
When disappointment, grief, and fear are gone.
Sorrow forgot, love's purest joys restored.
Be still, my soul; when change and tears are past,
All safe and blessed we shall meet at last.

Be Thou My Vision

Traditional Irish

Strum Pattern: 8
Pick Pattern: 8

Verse
Moderately

1. Be Thou my ___ vi - sion, oh Lord of my heart.
2., 3., 4. *See Additional Lyrics*

Naught be all else to me, save that Thou art.

Thou my ___ best ___ thought, ___ by day or by night, ___ wak - ing or

sleep - ing, Thy ___ pres - ence my light. all.

Additional Lyrics

2. Be Thou my wisdom, and Thou my true word.
   I ever with Thee and Thou with me, Lord.
   Thou my great Father, I Thy true son,
   Thou in me dwelling, and I with Thee one.

3. Riches I heed not, nor man's empty praise.
   Thou mine inheritance, now and always.
   Thou and Thou only, first in my heart,
   High King of heaven, my treasure Thou art.

4. High King of heaven, my victory won.
   May I reach heaven's joys, oh bright heav'n's sun!
   Heart of my own heart, whatever befall,
   Still be my vision, oh Ruler of all.

The Beautiful Garden of Prayer

Words by Eleanor Allen Schroll
Music by James H. Fillmore

Strum Pattern: 8
Pick Pattern: 8

Additional Lyrics

2. There's a garden where Jesus is waiting,
   And I go, with my burden and care.
   Just to learn from His lips words of comfort
   In the beautiful garden of prayer.

3. There's a garden where Jesus is waiting,
   And He bids you to come meet Him there,
   Just to bow and receive a new blessing
   In the beautiful garden of prayer.

Beautiful Savior

Words from *Gesangbuch*
Music adapted from Silesian Folk Tune

Strum Pattern: 4
Pick Pattern: 3

Verse
Moderately

1. Beau - ti - ful Sav - ior, King of cre - a - tion,
2., 3., 4. *See Additional Lyrics*

Son of _____ God and _____ Son of Man!

Tru - ly I'd love _____ thee, tru - ly I'd serve _____ thee,

Light of my soul, my joy, my crown. thine!

Additional Lyrics

2. Fair are the meadows, fair are the woodlands,
   Robed in flow'rs of blooming spring.
   Jesus is fairer, Jesus is purer,
   He makes our sorrowing spirit sing.

3. Fair is the sunshine, fair is the moonlight,
   Bright the sparkling stars on high.
   Jesus shines brighter, Jesus shines purer
   Than all the angels in the sky.

4. Beautiful Savior, Lord of the nations,
   Son of God and Son of Man!
   Glory and honor, praise, adoration,
   Now and forevermore be thine!

Beneath the Cross of Jesus

Words by Elizabeth C. Clephane
Music by Frederick C. Maker

Strum Pattern: 3
Pick Pattern: 3

1. Be - neath the cross of Je - sus, I fain would take my stand, the
2. *See Additional Lyrics*

shad - ow of a might - y rock with - in a wea - ry land. A

home with - in the wild - er - ness, a rest up - on the way, from the

burn - ing of the noon - tide heat and the bur - den of the day. 2. Up - ness.

Additional Lyrics

2. Upon the cross of Jesus, mine eyes at times can see
The very dying form of One who suffered there for me.
And from my sticken heart, with tears, two wonders I confess:
The wonders of redeeming love and my unworthiness.

Blessed Assurance

Lyrics by Fanny Crosby and Van Alstyne
Music by Phoebe P. Knapp

Strum Pattern: 8
Pick Pattern: 8

Verse
Moderately

1. Bles - sed as - sur - ance, Je - sus is mine! _____ Oh, what a
2., 3. *See Additional Lyrics*

fore - taste of glo - ry di - vine! _____ Heir of sal - va - tion,

pur - chase of God, _____ born of His spir - it, washed in His blood. _____

Chorus

This is my sto - ry, this is my song, _____ prais - ing my Sav -

ior all the day long. _____ This is my sto - ry, this is my

song, _____ prais - ing my Sav - ior all the day long. _____

Additional Lyrics

2. Perfect submission, perfect delight,
Visions of rapture now burst on my sight.
Angels descending, bring from above
Echoes of mercy, whispers of love.

3. Perfect submission, all is at rest.
I in my Savior am happy and blest.
Watching and waiting, looking above,
Filled with His goodness, lost in His love.

Breathe on Me, Breath of God

Words by Edwin Hatch
Music by Robert Jackson

Strum Pattern: 8
Pick Pattern: 8

Verse
Moderately

1. Breathe on me, breath of God. Fill me with life a-new,
2., 3., 4. *See Additional Lyrics*

that I may love what dost Thou love and do ___ what Thou wouldst do. ty.

Additional Lyrics

2. Breathe on me, breath of God,
   Until my heart is pure,
   Until with Thee, I will one will,
   To do and to endure.

3. Breathe on me, breath of God,
   Till I am wholly Thine,
   Until this earthly part of me
   Glows with Thy fire divine.

4. Breathe on me, breath of God,
   So shall I never die,
   But live with Thee, the perfect life
   Of thine eternity.

Children of the Heavenly Father

Words by Simon Browne
Music by William Knapp

Strum Pattern: 8
Pick Pattern: 8

Verse
Moderately

1. Chil-dren of the heav'n-ly Fa-ther safe-ly in His bo-som gath-er; nest-ling
2., 3., 4. *See Additional Lyrics*

bird or star in heav-en such a ref-uge ne'er was giv-en. 2. God His ho-ly.

Additional Lyrics

2. God His own doth tend and nourish,
   In His holy courts they flourish.
   From all evil things He spares them,
   In His mighty arms He bears them.

3. Neither life nor death shall ever
   From the Lord His children sever;
   Unto them His grace He showeth,
   And their sorrows all He knoweth.

4. Though He giveth or He taketh,
   God His children ne'er forsaketh;
   His the loving purpose solely
   To preserve them pure and holy.

Bringing in the Sheaves

Words by Knowles Shaw
Music by George A. Minor

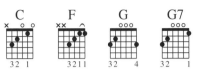

Strum Pattern: 2, 3
Pick Pattern: 3, 4

Additional Lyrics

2. Sowing in the sunshine, sowing in the shadows,
   Fearing neither clouds nor winter's chilling breeze.
   By and by the harvest and the labor ended,
   We shall come rejoicing, bringing in the sheaves.

3. Going forth with weeping, sowing for the Master,
   Though the loss sustained our spirit often grieves.
   When our weeping's over, He will bid us welcome,
   We shall come rejoicing, bringing in the sheaves.

A Child of the King

Traditional

Strum Pattern: 8, 9
Pick Pattern: 8, 9

Additional Lyrics

2. My Father's own Son, the Savior of men,
   Once wandered on earth as the poorest of them.
   But now He is reigning forever on high,
   And will give me a home in the heav'n by and by.

3. I once was an outcast stranger on earth,
   A sinner by choice and an alien by birth.
   But I've been adopted; my name's written down,
   An heir to a mansion, a robe and a crown.

4. A tent or a cottage, why should I care?
   They're building a palace for me over there.
   Though exiled from home, yet still I may sing:
   "All glory to God, I'm a child of the King."

The Church's One Foundation

Words by Samuel Stone
Music by Samuel Wesley

Strum Pattern: 4
Pick Pattern: 1

Verse
Moderately

1. The church-'s one foun-da-tion is Je-sus Christ her Lord. She
2., 3. *See Additional Lyrics*

is His new cre-a-tion, by wa-ter and the Word. From

heav'n He came and sought her to be His ho-ly bride, with

His own blood He bought her, and for her life He died. 2. E - rest.

Additional Lyrics

2. Elect from ev'ry nation, yet one o'er all the earth.
   Her charter of salvation, one Lord, one faith, one birth.
   One holy name she blesses, partakes one holy food,
   And to one hope she presses, with ev'ry grace endued.

3. 'Mid toil and tribulation, and tumult of her war,
   She waits the consumation of peace forevermore.
   Till with the vision glorious, her longing eyes are blest,
   And the great church victorious shall be the church at rest.

Close to Thee

Words by Fanny J. Crosby
Music by Silas J. Vail

Strum Pattern: 8
Pick Pattern: 8

Additional Lyrics

2. Not for ease or worldly pleasure,
   Nor for fame my prayer shall be;
   Gladly will I toil and suffer,
   Only let me walk with Thee.

Chorus 2. Close to Thee, close to Thee,
   Close to Thee, close to Thee;
   Gladly will I toil and suffer,
   Only let me walk with Thee.

3. Lead me through the vail of shadows,
   Bear me o'er life's fitful sea;
   Then the gate of life eternal,
   May I enter, Lord, with Thee.

Chorus 3. Close to Thee, close to Thee,
   Close to Thee, close to Thee;
   Then the gate of life eternal,
   May I enter, Lord, with Thee.

Come Christians Join to Sing

Words by Christian Henry Bateman
Traditional Melody

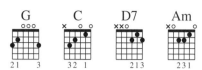

Strum Pattern: 2
Pick Pattern: 2

Additional Lyrics

2. Come lift your hearts on high,
Alleluia! Amen!
Let praises fill the sky;
Alleluia! Amen!
He is our guide and friend;
To us He'll condescend;
His love shall never end:
Alleluia! Amen!

3. Praise yet our Christ again,
Alleluia! Amen!
Life shall not end the strain;
Alleluia! Amen!
On heaven's blissful shore
His goodness we'll adore,
Singing forevermore,
"Alleluia! Amen!"

Come, Thou Almighty King

Anonymous Text
Music by Felice de Giardini

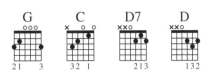

Strum Pattern: 8
Pick Pattern: 8

Additional Lyrics

2. Come, Thou incarnate Word,
Gird on Thy mighty sword;
Our pray'r attend;
Come, and Thy people bless,
And give Thy word success,
Spirit of holiness,
On us descend.

3. Come, holy Comforter!
Thy sacred witness bear,
In this glad hour;
Thou who almighty art,
Now rule in ev'ry heart,
And ne'er from us depart,
Spirit of pow'r!

4. To the great One in Three,
The highest praises be,
Hence evermore!
His sov'reign majesty
May we in glory see,
And to eternity
Love and adore.

Come, Thou Fount of Every Blessing

Words by Robert Robinson
Traditional Music compiled by John Wyeth

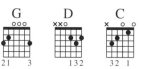

Strum Pattern: 8
Pick Pattern: 8

1. Come, Thou fount of ev'ry bless-ing, tune my heart to sing Thy grace, streams of
2., 3. *See Additional Lyrics*

mer-cy, nev-er ceas-ing call for songs of loud-est praise. Teach me

some me-lo-dious son-net, sung by flam-ing tongues a-bove. Praise the

mount! I'm fixed up-on it, mount of Thy re-deem-ing love. 2. Here I bove.

Additional Lyrics

2. Here I raise mine Ebenezer,
   Hither by Thy help I'm come.
   And I hope, by Thy good pleasure,
   Safely to arrive at home.
   Jesus sought me when a stranger,
   Wand'ring from the fold of God;
   He, to rescue me from danger,
   Interposed His precious blood.

3. Oh, to grace how great a debtor
   Daily I'm constrained to be!
   Let Thy grace, Lord, like a fetter,
   Bind my wand'ring heart to Thee.
   Prone to wander, Lord I feel it,
   Prone to leave the God I love;
   Here's my heart, Lord, take and seal it,
   Seal it for Thy courts above.

Come, Ye Sinners

Words by Joseph Hart
Traditional Music

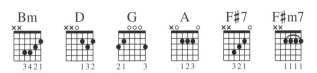

Strum Pattern: 1, 3
Pick Pattern: 2, 4

Verse
Moderately Slow

1. Come, ye sin - ners, _ poor and need - y, weak and wound - ed, _ sick and sore;
2., 3., 4. *See Additional Lyrics*

Je - sus read - y stands to save _ you, full of pit - y, _ love and pow'r.

Chorus

I will a - rise and _ go to Je - sus, He will em - brace me _

in His arms; in the arms of my dear Sav - ior,

1., 2., 3.

O, there are _ ten _ thou - sand charms.

4.

thou - sand charms. _

Additional Lyrics

2. Come, ye thirsty, come, and welcome,
   God's free bounty glorify;
   True belief and true repentance,
   Ev'ry grace that brings you nigh.

3. Let not conscience make you linger,
   Nor of fitness fondly dream;
   All the fitness He requireth
   Is to feel your need of Him.

4. Come, ye weary, heavy laden,
   Lost and ruined by the fall;
   If you tarry till you're better
   You will never come at all.

Come, Ye Thankful People, Come

Words by Henry Alford
Music by George Job Elvey

Strum Pattern: 4
Pick Pattern: 1

Additional Lyrics

2. All the world is God's own field,
   Fruit unto his praise to yield;
   Wheat and tares together sown,
   Unto joy or sorrow grown.
   First the blade, and then the ear,
   Then the full corn shall appear.
   Grant, O harvest Lord, that we
   Wholesome grain and pure may be.

3. For the Lord our God shall come,
   And shall take His harvest-home;
   From his field shall in that day
   All offenses purge away.
   Give his angels change at last
   In the fire the tares to cast,
   But the fruitful ears to store
   In His garner evermore.

4. Even so, Lord, quickly come
   To Thy final harvest-home;
   Gather Thou thy people in,
   Free from sorrow, free from sin.
   There forever purified,
   In Thy presence to abide.
   Come, with all Thine angels come,
   Raise the glorious harvest-home.

Count Your Blessings

Words by Johnson Oatman, Jr.
Music by Edwin O. Excell

Strum Pattern: 10
Pick Pattern: 10

Additional Lyrics

2. Are you ever burdened with a load of care?
Does the cross seem heavy you are called to bear?
Count your many blessings; ev'ry doubt will fly.
And you will be singing as the days go by.

3. When you look at others with their lands and gold,
Think that Christ has promised you His wealth untold;
Count your many blessings; money cannot buy
Your reward in heaven nor your home on high.

4. So amid the conflict, whether great or small,
Do not be discouraged, God is over all.
Count your many blessings; angels will attend.
Help and comfort give you to your journey's end.

Christ the Lord Is Risen Today

Words by Charles Wesley
Music adapted from *Lyra Davidica*

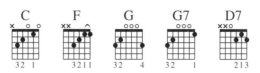

Strum Pattern: 2, 3
Pick Pattern: 3, 4

Verse
Brightly

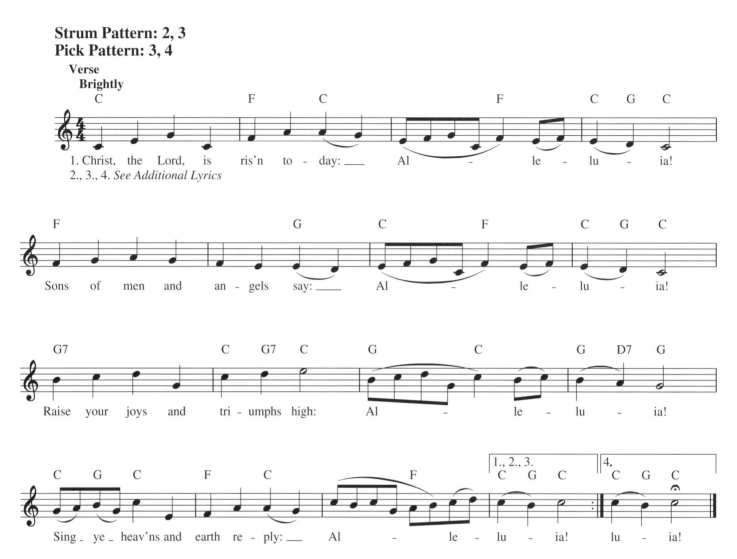

1. Christ, the Lord, is ris'n to - day: ___ Al - le - lu - ia!
2., 3., 4. *See Additional Lyrics*

Sons of men and an - gels say: ___ Al - le - lu - ia!

Raise your joys and tri - umphs high: Al - le - lu - ia!

Sing ye heav'ns and earth re - ply: ___ Al - le - lu - ia! lu - ia!

Additional Lyrics

2. Lives again our glorious King: Alleluia!
   Where, O death, is now thy sting? Alleluia!
   Dying once, He all doth save: Alleluia!
   Where thy victory, O grave? Alleluia!

3. Love's redeeming work is done, Alleluia!
   Fought the fight, the battle won: Alleluia!
   Death in vain forbids Him rise: Alleluia!
   Christ has opened Paradise. Alleluia!

4. Soar we now, where Christ has led, Alleluia!
   Foll'wing our exalted Head: Alleluia!
   Made like Him, like Him we rise: Alleluia!
   Ours the cross, the grave, the skies. Alleluia!

Dear Lord and Father of Mankind

Words by John Greenleaf Whittier
Music by Frederick Charles Maker

Strum Pattern: 3, 4
Pick Pattern: 1, 3

Additional Lyrics

2. In simple trust like theirs who heard,
   Beside the Syrian Sea,
   The gracious calling of the Lord,
   Let us, like them, without a word
   Rise up and follow Thee.

3. O Sabbath rest by Galilee,
   O calm of hills above.
   Where Jesus knelt to share with Thee
   The silence of eternity,
   Interpreted by love!

4. Drop Thy still dews of quietness,
   Till all our strivings cease.
   Take from our souls the strain and stress,
   And let our ordered lives confess
   The beauty of Thy peace.

5. Breathe through the heats of our desire,
   Thy coolness and Thy balm;
   Let sense be dumb, let flesh retire,
   Speak through the earthquake, wind and fire,
   O still small voice of calm!

Fairest Lord Jesus

Words for stanza 4 by Joseph August Seiss
Music from *Schlesische Volkslieder*
Arranged by Richard Storrs Willis

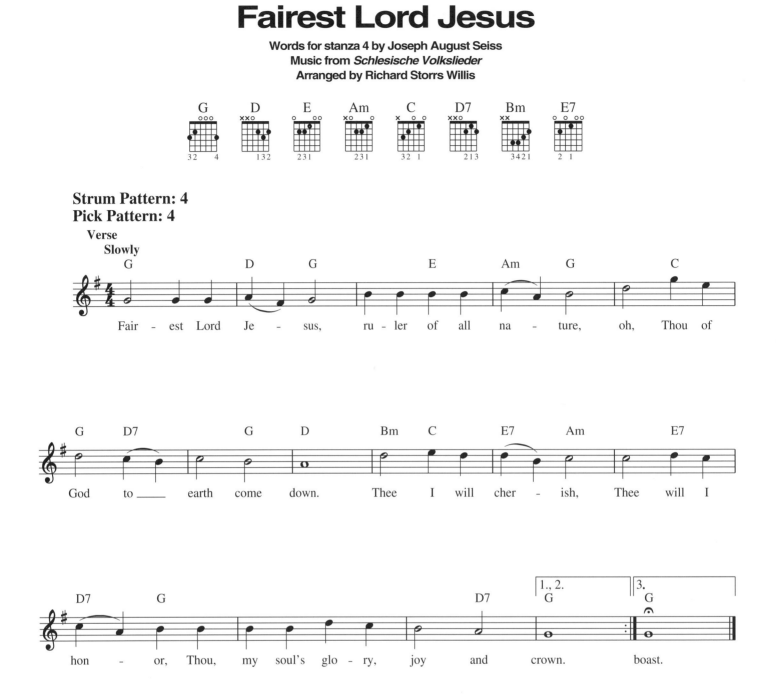

Strum Pattern: 4
Pick Pattern: 4

Verse
Slowly

Fair - est Lord Je - sus, ru - ler of all na - ture, oh, Thou of

God to _____ earth come down. Thee I will cher - ish, Thee will I

hon - or, Thou, my soul's glo - ry, joy and crown. boast.

Additional Lyrics

2. Fair are the meadows, fairer still the woodlands,
   Robed in the blooming garb of spring.
   Jesus is fairer, Jesus is purer,
   Who makes the woeful heart to sing.

3. Fair is the sunshine, fairer still the moonlight,
   And the twinkling, starry host.
   Jesus shines brighter, Jesus shines purer
   Then all the angels heaven can boast.

4. Beautiful Savior! Lord of the nations!
   Son of God and Son of man!
   Glory and honor, praise, adoration,
   Now and forevermore be Thine!

Faith of Our Fathers

Words by Frederick W. Faber
Music by Henri F. Hemy and James G. Walton

Strum Pattern: 7
Pick Pattern: 9

Additional Lyrics

2. Our fathers, chained in prisons dark,
   Were still in heart and conscience free.
   How sweet would be their children's fate,
   If they, like them, should die for thee.

3. Faith of our fathers! We will love
   Both friend and foe in all our strife.
   And preach thee, too, as love knows how,
   By kindly words and virtuous life.

Footsteps of Jesus

Words by Mary B.C. Slade
Music by Asa B. Everett

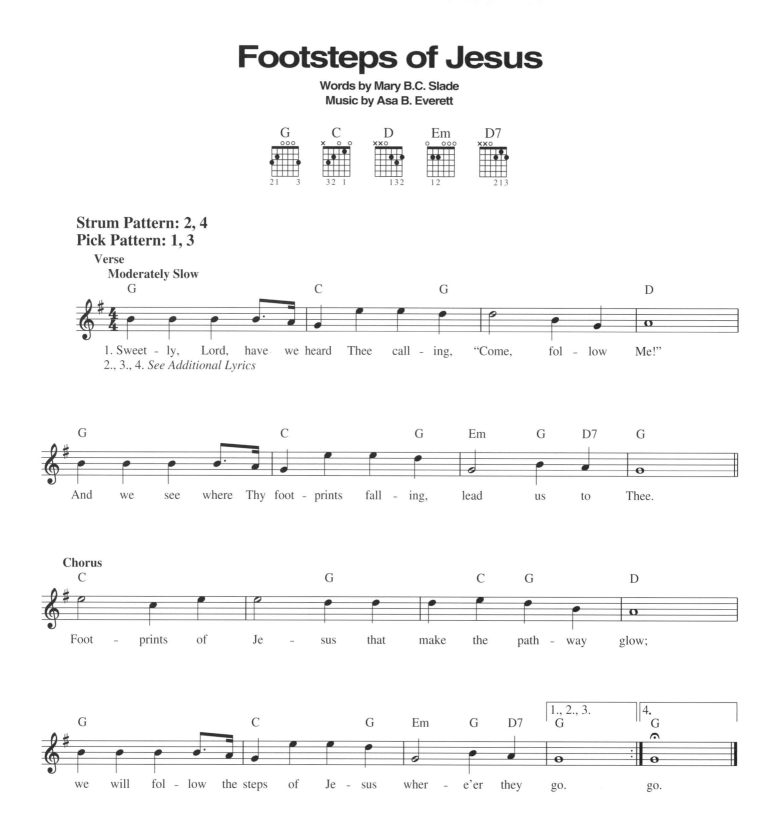

Strum Pattern: 2, 4
Pick Pattern: 1, 3

Verse
Moderately Slow

1. Sweet - ly, Lord, have we heard Thee call - ing, "Come, fol - low Me!"
2., 3., 4. *See Additional Lyrics*

And we see where Thy foot - prints fall - ing, lead us to Thee.

Chorus

Foot - prints of Je - sus that make the path - way glow;

we will fol - low the steps of Je - sus wher - e'er they go. go.

Additional Lyrics

2. Though they lead o'er the cold, dark mountains, seeking His sheep,
   Or along by Siloam's fountains, helping the weak.

3. If they lead through the temple holy, preaching the Word,
   Or in homes of the poor and lowly, serving the Lord.

4. Then at last, when on high he sees us, our journey done,
   We will rest where the steps of Jesus end at His throne.

For All the Saints

Text by William W. How
Music by R. Vaughan Williams

Strum Pattern: 4
Pick Pattern: 1

Verse
Slowly

1. For all the saints who from their la - bors rest,
2. – 6. *See Additional Lyrics*

who Thee by faith be - fore the world con - fessed, Thy

name, O Je - sus, be for - ev - er _____ blest. Al -

- le - lu - ia! Al - le - lu - ia! ia!

Additional Lyrics

2. Thou wast their Rock, their Fortress, and their Might;
Thou, Lord, their Captain in the well-fought fight;
Thou, in the darkness drear, their one true Light.
Alleluia! Alleluia!

3. O may Thy soldiers, faithful, true and bold,
Fight as the saints who nobly fought of old,
And win with them the victor's crown of gold.
Alleluia! Alleluia!

4. O blest communion, fellowship divine!
We feebly struggle, they in glory shine;
Yet all are one in Thee, for all are Thine.
Alleluia! Alleluia!

5. But lo! There breaks a yet more glorious day:
The saints triumphant rise in bright array;
The King of Glory passes on His way.
Alleluia! Alleluia!

6. From earth's wide bounds, from ocean's farthest coast,
Through gates of pearl streams in the countless host,
Singing to Father, Son and Holy Ghost:
Alleluia! Alleluia!

For the Beauty of the Earth

Text by Folliot S. Pierpoint
Music by Conrad Kocher

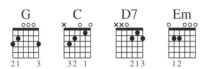

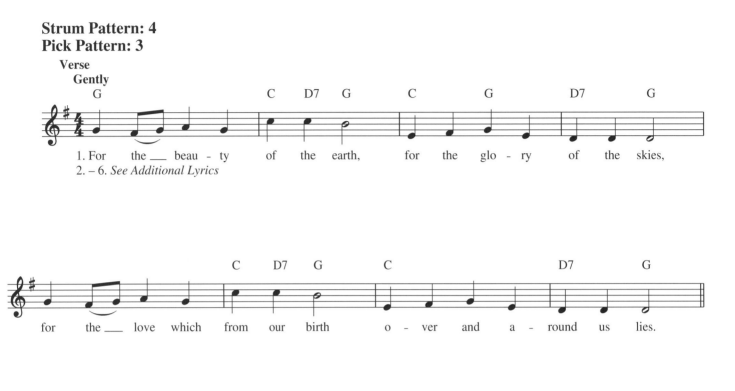

Strum Pattern: 4
Pick Pattern: 3

1. For the __ beau-ty of the earth, for the glo-ry of the skies,
2. – 6. *See Additional Lyrics*

for the __ love which from our birth o-ver and a-round us lies.

Lord of all, to Thee we raise this our hymn of grate-ful praise. grate-ful praise.

Additional Lyrics

2. For the beauty of each hour
   Of the day and of the night,
   Hill and vale, and tree and flower,
   Sun and moon and stars of light.

3. For the joy of ear and eye,
   For the heart and mind's delight,
   For the mystic harmony
   Linking sense to sound and sight.

4. For the joy of human love,
   Brother, sister, parent, child,
   Friends on earth and friends above,
   For all gentle thoughts and mild.

5. For Thy church that evermore
   Lifteth holy hands above,
   Offering upon every shore
   Her pure sacrifice of love.

6. For Thy self, best Gift Divine,
   To the world so freely given,
   For that great, great love of Thine,
   Peace on earth and joy in heaven.

Optional Chorus for Holy Communion

Christ, our God, to Thee we raise
This our sacrifice of praise.

Give Me Jesus

African-American Spiritual

Strum Pattern: 8
Pick Pattern: 8

Additional Lyrics

2. Take the world, but give me Jesus;
   Sweetest comfort of my soul.
   With my Savior watching o'er me,
   I can sing though billows roll.

3. Take the world, but give me Jesus;
   Let me view His constant smile.
   Then throughout my pilgrim journey
   Light will cheer me all the while.

4. Take the world, but give me Jesus;
   In His cross my trust shall be,
   Till, with clearer, brighter vision,
   Face to face my Lord I see.

Give Me That Old Time Religion

Traditional

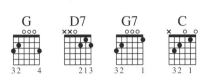

Strum Pattern: 3
Pick Pattern: 2, 5

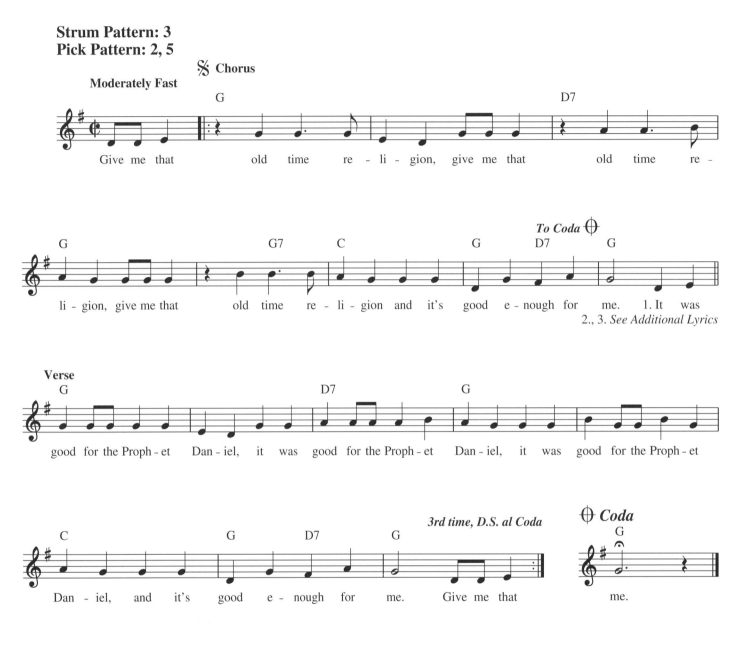

Additional Lyrics

2. It was good for Paul and Silas,
   It was good for Paul and Silas,
   It was good for Paul and Silas,
   And it's good enough for me.

3. It was good for old Abe Lincoln,
   It was good for old Abe Lincoln,
   It was good for old Abe Lincoln,
   And it's good enough for me.

Glory to His Name

Words by Elisha A. Hoffman
Music by John H. Stockton

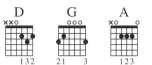

Strum Pattern: 3, 4
Pick Pattern: 1, 3

Additional Lyrics

2. I am so wondrously saved from sin,
   Jesus so sweetly abides within;
   There at the cross where He took me in;
   Glory to His name!

3. O precious fountain that saves from sin,
   I am so glad that I entered in;
   There Jesus saves me and keeps me clean;
   Glory to His name!

4. Come to this fountain so rich and sweet;
   Cast thy poor soul at the Savior's feet;
   Plunge in today and be made complete;
   Glory to His name!

God of Grace and God of Glory

Text by Harry Emerson Fosdick
Music by John Hughes

Strum Pattern: 2
Pick Pattern: 2

Verse
Moderately

1. God of grace and God of glory, on Thy people
2., 3., 4. *See Additional Lyrics*

pour Thy power. Crown Thine an - cient Church's sto - ry, bring her bud to

glo - rious flower. Grant us wis - dom, grant us cour - age, for the fac - ing of this

hour, for the fac - ing of this hour. man nor Thee.

Additional Lyrics

2. Lo! The hosts of evil round us
   Scorn Thy Christ, assail His ways!
   From the fears that long have bound us,
   Free our hearts to faith and praise.
   Grant us wisdom, grant us courage,
   For the living of these days,
   For the living of these days.

3. Cure Thy children's warring madness,
   Bend our pride to Thy control.
   Shame our wanton, selfish gladness,
   Rich in things and poor in soul.
   Grant us wisdom, grant us courage,
   Lest we miss Thy Kingdom's goal,
   Lest we miss Thy Kingdom's goal.

4. Set our feet on lofty places,
   Gird our lives that they may be
   Armored with all Christ-like graces
   In the fight to set men free.
   Grant us wisdom, grant us courage,
   That we fail not man nor Thee,
   That we fail not man nor Thee.

God of Our Fathers

Words by Daniel C. Roberts
Music by George W. Warren

Strum Pattern: 2, 5
Pick Pattern: 1, 2

Verse
Majestically

1. God of our fa - thers, Whose al - might - y hand
2., 3., 4. *See Additional Lyrics*

leads forth in beau - ty all the star - ry band

of shin - ing worlds in splen - dor through the skies,

our grate - ful songs be - fore Thy throne a - rise. Thine!

Additional Lyrics

2. Thy love divine hath led us in the past.
   In this free land by Thee our lot is cast.
   Be Thou our ruler, guardian, guide and stay;
   Thy word our law, Thy paths our chosen way.

3. From war's alarms, from deadly pestilence,
   Be Thy strong arm our ever-sure defense.
   Thy true religion in our hearts increase,
   Thy bounteous goodness nourish us in peace.

4. Refresh Thy people on their toilsome way,
   Lead us from night to never-ending day.
   Fill all our lives with love and grace divine,
   And glory laud, and praise forever Thine!

Have Thine Own Way Lord

Words by Adelaide Pollard
Music by George Stebbins

A   D   E   E6   E7   A7

Strum Pattern: 8
Pick Pattern: 8

Verse

Moderately

1. Have Thine own way, Lord! Have Thine own way! Thou art the
2., 3. *See Additional Lyrics*

Pot - ter, I am the clay. Mold me and make me af - ter Thy

will, while I am wait - ing, yield-ed and still. 2. Have Thine own me!

Additional Lyrics

2. Have Thine own way, Lord! Have Thine own way!
Search me and try me, Master, today!
Whiter than snow, Lord, wash me just now,
As in Thy presence humbly I bow.

3. Have Thine own way, Lord! Have Thine own way!
Hold o'er my being absolute sway!
Fill with Thy spirit till all shall see
Christ only, always, living in me!

I Have Decided to Follow Jesus

Words by an Indian Prince
Musc by Auila Read

G   D7   G7   C   A7

Strum Pattern: 6
Pick Pattern: 4

Verse

Moderately Slow

1. I have de - cid - ed to fol - low Je - sus. I have de -
2., 3. *See Additional Lyrics*

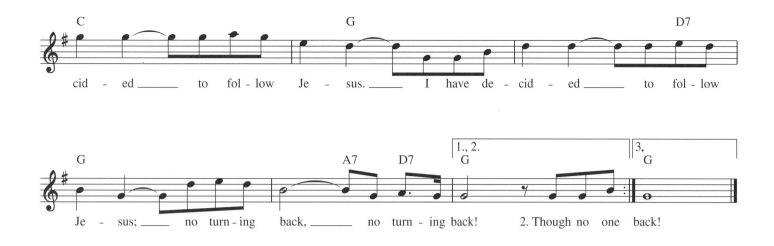

cid - ed _____ to fol - low Je - sus. _____ I have de - cid - ed _____ to fol - low

Je - sus; _____ no turn - ing back, _____ no turn - ing back! 2. Though no one back!

Additional Lyrics

2. Though no one join me, still I will follow.
Though no one join me, still I will follow.
Though no one join me, still I will follow;
No turning back, no turning back!

3. The world behind me, the cross before me;
The world behind me, the cross before me;
The world behind me, the cross before me;
No turning back, no turning back!

In Christ There Is No East or West

Words by John Oxenham
Music by Alexander Robert Reinagle

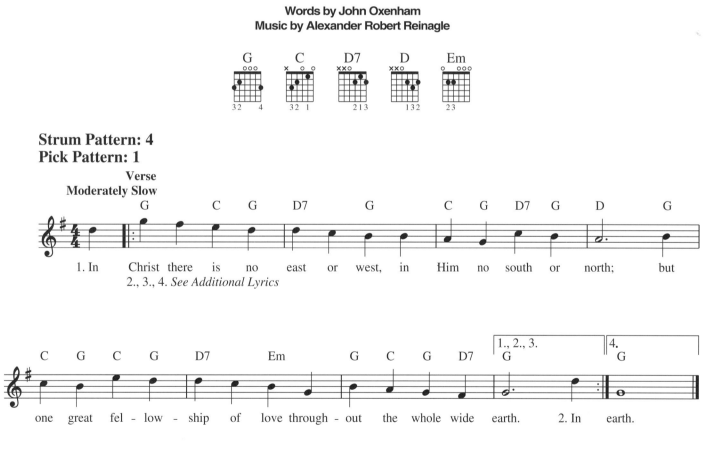

Strum Pattern: 4
Pick Pattern: 1

Verse
Moderately Slow

1. In Christ there is no east or west, in Him no south or north; but
2., 3., 4. *See Additional Lyrics*

one great fel - low - ship of love through - out the whole wide earth. 2. In earth.

Additional Lyrics

2. In Christ shall true hearts ev'rywhere
Their high communion find;
His service is the golden cord
Close-binding humankind.

3. Join hands, disciples of the faith,
Whate'er your race may be.
All children of the living God
Are surely kin to me.

4. In Christ now meet both east and west,
In Him meet south and north;
All Christly souls are one in Him
Throughout the whole wide earth.

He Hideth My Soul

Words by Fanny J. Crosby
Music by William J. Kirkpatrick

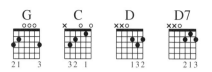

Strum Pattern: 8, 9
Pick Pattern: 8, 9

Additional Lyrics

2. A wonderful Savior is Jesus my Lord,
   He taketh my burden away.
   He holdeth me up and I shall not be moved.
   He giveth me strength as my day.

3. With numberless blessings, each moment He crowns
   And filled with His fullness divine,
   I sing in my rapture, oh glory to God
   For such a Redeemer as mine!

4. When clothed in His brightness, transported I rise
   To meet Him in clouds of the sky.
   His perfect salvation, His wonderful love,
   I'll shout with the millions on high.

He Keeps Me Singing

Words and Music by Luther B. Bridgers

Strum Pattern: 2, 3
Pick Pattern: 3, 4

Additional Lyrics

2. All my life was wrecked by sin and strife;
   Discord filled my heart with pain.
   Jesus swept across the broken strings,
   Stirred the slumb'ring chords again.

3. Feasting on the riches of His grace,
   Resting 'neath his shelt'ring wing,
   Always looking on His smiling face;
   That is why I shout and sing:

4. Though sometimes He leads through waters deep,
   Trials fall across the way.
   Though sometimes the path seems rough and steep,
   See His footprints all the way.

5. Soon He's coming back to welcome me
   Far beyond the starry sky.
   I shall wing my flight to worlds unknown;
   I shall reign with Him on high.

He's Got the Whole World in His Hands

African-American Folksong

Strum Pattern: 3, 4
Pick Pattern: 1, 3

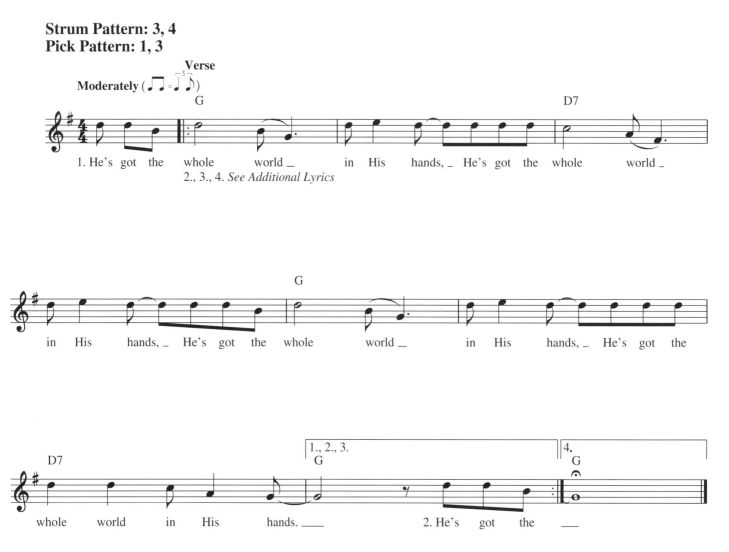

1. He's got the whole world ___ in His hands, ___ He's got the whole world ___
2., 3., 4. *See Additional Lyrics*

in His hands, ___ He's got the whole world ___ in His hands, ___ He's got the

whole world in His hands. ___ 2. He's got the ___

Additional Lyrics

2. He's got the wind and the rain in His hands,
   He's got the wind and the rain in His hands,
   He's got the wind and the rain in His hands,
   He's got the whole world in His hands.

3. He's got the tiny little baby in His hands,
   He's got the tiny little baby in His hands,
   He's got the tiny little baby in His hands,
   He's got the whole world in His hands.

4. He's got you and me, brother, in His hands,
   He's got you and me, sister, in His hands,
   He's got you and me, brother, in His hands,
   He's got the whole world in His hands.

Higher Ground

Words by Johnson Oatman, Jr.
Music by Charles H. Gabriel

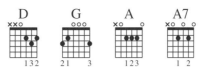

Strum Pattern: 8
Pick Pattern: 8

1. I'm press-ing on the up-ward way, new heights I'm gain-ing ev-'ry
2., 3., 4. *See Additional Lyrics*

day; still pray-ing as I'm on-ward bound, "Lord, plant my feet on high-er ground." Lord, lift me

up and let me stand by faith on heav-en's ta-ble-land; a high-er

plane than I have found, Lord, plant my feet on high-er ground. 2. My heart has ground."

Additional Lyrics

2. My heart has no desire to stay
   Where doubts arise and fears dismay;
   Though some may dwell where these abound,
   My prayer, my aim, is higher ground.

3. I want to live above the world,
   Though Satan's darts at me are hurled;
   For faith has caught the joyful sound,
   The song of saints on higher ground.

4. I want to scale the utmost height
   And catch a gleam of glory bright;
   But still I'll pray till heav'n I've found,
   "Lord, lead me on to higher ground."

Holy, Holy, Holy

Text by Reginald Heber
Music by John B. Dykes

Strum Pattern: 3
Pick Pattern: 3

Additional Lyrics

2. Holy, holy, holy! All the saints adore Thee.
   Casting down their golden crowns around the glassy sea.
   Cherubim and seraphim falling down before Thee,
   Which wert, and art, and evermore shall be.

3. Holy, holy, holy! Though the darkness hide Thee.
   Though the eye of sinful man Thy glory may not see.
   Only Thou art holy; there is none beside Thee,
   Perfect in power, in love and purity.

4. Holy, holy, holy! Lord God Almighty!
   All Thy works shall praise Thy name in earth and sky and sea.
   Holy, holy, holy! Merciful and mighty!
   God in three persons, blessed Trinity.

How Firm a Foundation

Traditional text compiled by John Rippon
Traditional music compiled by Joseph Funk

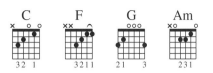

Strum Pattern: 2
Pick Pattern: 4

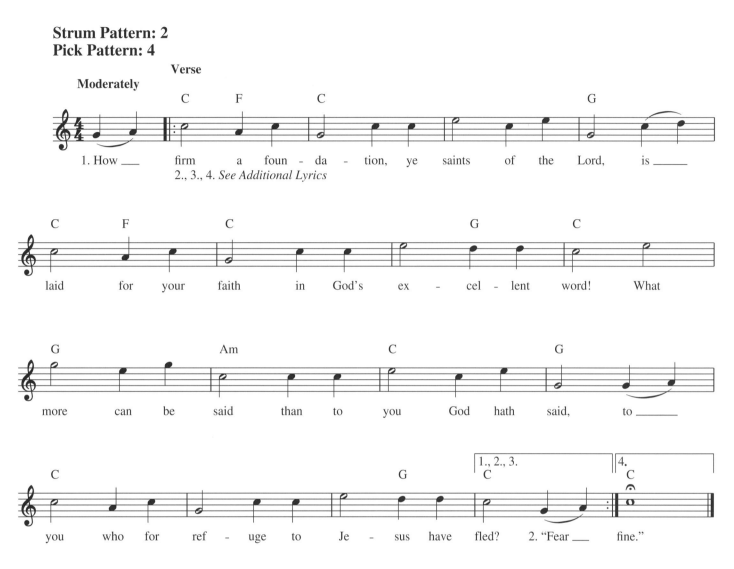

Additional Lyrics

2. "Fear not, I am with thee, oh be not dismayed,
   For I am thy God and will still give thee aid.
   I'll strengthen thee, help thee and cause thee to stand,
   Upheld by My righteous, omnipotent hand."

3. "When through the deep waters I call thee to go,
   The rivers of sorrow shall not overflow;
   For I will be near thee, thy troubles to bless,
   And sanctify to thee thy deepest distress."

4. "When through fiery trials, thy pathway shall lie,
   My grace, all sufficient, shall be thy supply.
   The flame shall not hurt thee; I only design
   Thy dross to consume and thy gold to refine."

I Am Resolved

Traditional

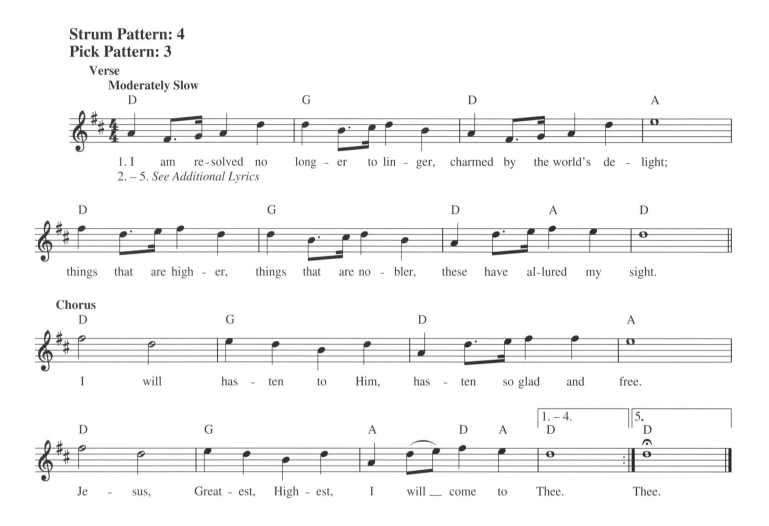

Strum Pattern: 4
Pick Pattern: 3

Verse
Moderately Slow

1. I am re-solved no long - er to lin - ger, charmed by the world's de - light;
2. – 5. *See Additional Lyrics*

things that are high - er, things that are no - bler, these have al - lured my sight.

Chorus

I will has - ten to Him, has - ten so glad and free.

Je - sus, Great - est, High - est, I will __ come to Thee. Thee.

Additional Lyrics

2. I am resolved to go to the Savior,
   Leaving my sin and strife.
   He is the true One; he is the just One;
   He hath the words of life.

3. I am resolved to follow the Savior,
   Faithful and true each day.
   Heed what He sayeth, do what He willeth;
   He is the Living Way.

4. I am resolved to enter the Kingdom,
   Leaving the paths of sin.
   Friends may oppose me, foes may beset me;
   Still will I enter in.

5. I am resolved, and who will go with me?
   Come, friends, without delay;
   Taught by the Bible, led by the Spirit,
   We'll walk the heav'nly way.

I Know a Fount

Words and Music by Oliver Cook

Strum Pattern: 4
Pick Pattern: 1, 3

Slowly

I know a fount where sins are washed a - way; I know a place where night is turned to day. Bur - dens are lift - ed; blind eyes made to see. There's a won - der - work - ing pow'r in the blood of Cal - va - ry.

I Love Thy Kingdom, Lord

Words by Tim Dwight
Music by Aaron Williams

Strum Pattern: 4
Pick Pattern: 4

Verse
Moderately Slow

1. I love Thy king - dom, Lord, the house of Thine a - bode. The
2., 3. *See Additional Lyrics*

church our blest re - deem - er saved with His own pre - cious blood. 2. I end.

Additional Lyrics

2. I love Thy church, oh, God!
   Her walls before Thee stand,
   Dear as the apple of Thine eye,
   And graven on Thy land.

3. For her my tears shall fall,
   For her my prayers ascend.
   To her my cares and toils be giv'n,
   Till toils and cares shall end.

I Know Whom I Have Believed

Words by Daniel Whittle
Music by James McGranahan

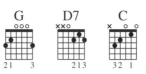

Strum Pattern: 6
Pick Pattern: 6

Additional Lyrics

2. I know not how the Spirit moves,
   Convincing men of sin,
   Revealing Jesus through the Word,
   Creating faith in Him.

3. I know now what of good or ill
   May be reserved for me,
   Of weary ways or golden days,
   Before His face I see.

4. I know not when my Lord may come,
   At night of noonday fair,
   Nor if I'll walk the vale* with Him,
   Or meet Him in the air.

*Valley of Death

I Love to Tell the Story

Words by Catherine Hankey
Music by William G. Fischer

Strum Pattern: 4
Pick Pattern: 4

Additional Lyrics

2. I love to tell the story; more wonderful it seems
   Than all the golden fancies of all our golden dreams.
   I love to tell the story; it did so much for me,
   And that is just the reason I tell it now to thee.

3. I love to tell the story; 'tis pleasant to repeat
   What seems each time I tell it, more wonderfully sweet.
   I love to tell the story, for some have never heard
   The message of salvation from God's own holy word.

4. I love to tell the story; for those who know it best
   Seem hungering and thirsting to hear it like the rest.
   And when, in scenes of glory, I sing the new, new song,
   'Twill be the old, old story that I have loved so long.

I Need Thee Every Hour

Words by Annie S. Hawks
Music by Robert Lowry

D A C E7 A7 G6

Strum Pattern: 9
Pick Pattern: 7

Verse
Moderately

1. I need Thee ev - 'ry hour, most gra - cious __ Lord; no
2., 3., 4. *See Additional Lyrics*

ten - der voice like Thine can peace _____ af - ford. I

Chorus

need Thee, O I need Thee; ev - 'ry hour I need Thee! O bless me now, my

Sav - ior: I come _____ to Thee! 2. I Thee! _____

1., 2., 3. **4.**

Additional Lyrics

2. I need Thee ev'ry hour, stay Thou nearby;
   Temptations lose their pow'r when Thou art nigh.

3. I need Thee ev'ry hour, in joy or pain;
   Come quickly and abide, or life is vain.

4. I need Thee ev'ry hour, Most Holy One;
   O make me Thine in deed, Thou blessed Son!

I Sing the Mighty Pow'r of God

Words by Isaac Watts
Traditional Music

Strum Pattern: 1, 3
Pick Pattern: 2, 4

Additional Lyrics

2. I sing the goodness of the Lord that filled the earth with food;
   God formed the creatures with a word and then pronounced them good.
   Lord, how Thy wonders are displayed, wher'er I turn my eyes;
   If I survey the ground I tread, or gaze upon the skies!

3. There's not a plant or flower below but makes Thy glories known;
   And clouds arise, and tempests blow, by order from Thy throne;
   While all that borrows life from Thee is ever in Thy care,
   And ev'rywhere that we can be, Thou, God, art present there.

I Surrender All

Words by J.W. Van Deventer
Music by W.S. Weeden

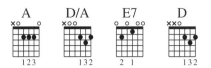

Strum Pattern: 3, 4
Pick Pattern: 2, 4

1. All to Je-sus I sur-ren-der; all to Him I free-ly give;
2. – 5. *See Additional Lyrics*

I will ev-er love and trust Him, in His pres-ence dai-ly live.

I sur-ren-der all, I sur-ren-der all,

all to Thee, my bless-ed Sav-ior, I sur-ren-der all. all.

Additional Lyrics

2. All to Jesus I surrender; humbly at His feet I bow,
   Worldly pleasures all forsaken; take me, Jesus, take me now.

3. All to Jesus I surrender; make me, Savior, wholly thine;
   Let me feel the Holy Spirit, truly know that Thou art mine.

4. All to Jesus I surrender; Lord, I give myself to Thee;
   Fill me with Thy love and power; let Thy blessing fall on me.

5. All to Jesus I surrender; now I feel the sacred flame.
   O the joy of full salvation! Glory, glory to His name!

I Want Jesus to Walk With Me

Traditional Spiritual

Additional Lyrics

2. In my trials, Lord, walk with me.
   In my trials, Lord, walk with me.
   When my heart is almost breaking,
   Lord, I want Jesus to walk with me.

3. When I'm troubled, Lord, walk with me.
   When I'm troubled, Lord, walk with me.
   When my head is bowed in sorrow
   Lord, I want Jesus to walk with me.

I Would Be True

Words by Howard A. Walter
Music by Joseph Y. Peek

Strum Pattern: 4
Pick Pattern: 1

Verse
Moderately Slow

1. I would be true, for there are those who trust me;
2. *See Additional Lyrics*

I would be pure, for there are those who care;

I would be strong, for there is much to suf - fer;

I would be brave, for there is much to dare,

I would be brave, for there is much to dare. lift.

Additional Lyrics

2. I would be friend of all,
   The foe, the friendless;
   I would be giving,
   And forget the gift,
   I would be humble,
   For I know my weakness;
   I would look up,
   And laugh and love and lift,
   I would look up,
   And laugh and love and lift.

In the Garden

Words and Music by C. Austin Miles

Strum Pattern: 8, 9
Pick Pattern: 8, 9

Verse
Moderately

1. I come to the gar - den a - lone, _____ while the
2., 3. *See Additional Lyrics*

dew is still on the ros - es, and the voice I hear fall - ing

on my ear, the Son of God dis - clos - es, and He

Chorus

walks with me and He talks with me, and He tells me

I am His own, _____ and the joy we share as we tar - ry

there, none oth - er has ev - er known. _____ 2. He _____

Additional Lyrics

2. He speaks, and the sound of His voice
Is so sweet the birds hush their singing,
And the melody that He gave to me
Within my heart is ringing.

3. I'd stay in the garden with Him,
Though the night around me be falling.
But He bids me go through the voice of woe;
His voice to me is calling.

Immortal, Invisible

Words by Walter Chalmers Smith
Traditional Music

Strum Pattern: 8
Pick Pattern: 8

Verse
Moderately

1. Im - mor - tal, in - vis - i - ble, God on - ly wise, in light in - ac -
2., 3., 4. *See Additional Lyrics*

ces - si - ble hid from our eyes. Most bless - ed most glo - rious, the an - cient of

days. Al - might - y, vic - to - rious, Thy great name we praise. 2. Un - Thee.

Additional Lyrics

2. Unresting, unhasting, and silent as light,
   Nor wanting, nor wasting, Thou rulest in might.
   Thy justice like mountains high soaring above
   Thy clouds, which are fountains of goodness and love.

3. To all, life Thou givest, to both great and small,
   In all life Thou livest, the true life of all.
   We blossom and flourish as leaves on the tree,
   And wither and perish but naught changeth Thee.

4. Great Father of glory, pure Father of light,
   Thine angels adore Thee, all veiling their sight.
   All praise we would render, Oh help us to see,
   'Tis only the splendor or light hideth Thee.

Kum Ba Yah

Traditional

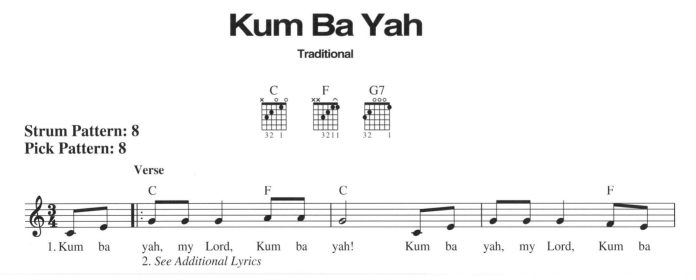

Strum Pattern: 8
Pick Pattern: 8

Verse

1. Kum ba yah, my Lord, Kum ba yah! Kum ba yah, my Lord, Kum ba
2. *See Additional Lyrics*

yah! Kum ba yah, my Lord, Kum ba yah! O Lord, — Kum ba

1. C
yah! 2. Some-one's yah!

2. C F C G7 C F C
yah! *Hum:* Mm. _____

Additional Lyrics

2. Someone's cryin', Lord, Kum ba yah!
Someone's cryin', Lord, Kum ba yah!
Someone's cryin', Lord, Kum ba yah!
O Lord, Kum ba yah!

My Faith Looks Up to Thee

Words by Ray Palmer
Music by Lowell Mason

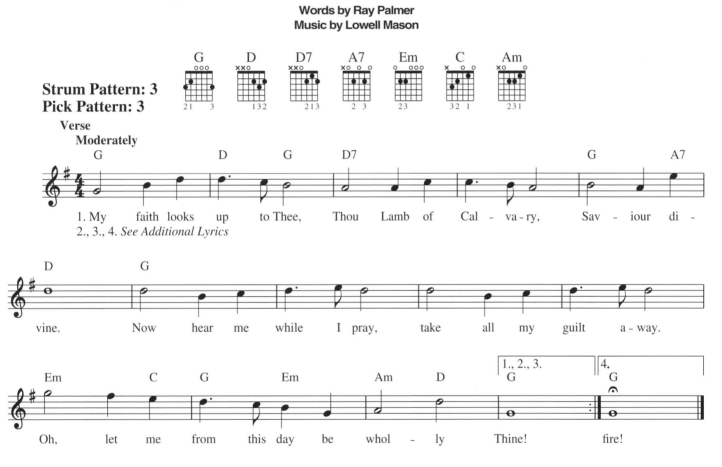

Strum Pattern: 3
Pick Pattern: 3

Verse
Moderately

1. My faith looks up to Thee, Thou Lamb of Cal - va - ry, Sav - iour di -
2., 3., 4. *See Additional Lyrics*

vine. Now hear me while I pray, take all my guilt a - way.

Oh, let me from this day be whol - ly Thine! fire!

Additional Lyrics

2. When ends life's transient dream,
When death's cold, sullen stream
Shall o'er me roll,
Blest Saviour, then, in love,
Fear and distrust remove.
Oh bear me safe above,
A ransomed soul!

3. While life's dark maze I tread,
And griefs around me spread,
Be Thou my guide.
Bid darkness turn to day,
Wipe sorrow's tears away,
Nor let me ever stray
From Thee aside.

4. May Thy rich grace impart
Strength to my fainting heart,
My zeal inspire.
As Thou hast died for me,
Oh may my love to Thee,
Pure, warm and changeless be,
A living fire!

In the Sweet By and By

Words by Sanford Fillmore Bennett
Music by Joseph P. Webster

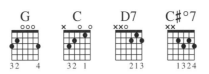

Strum Pattern: 2, 3
Pick Pattern: 3, 4

Additional Lyrics

2. We shall sing on that beautiful shore
   The melodious songs of the blest.
   And our spirits shall sorrow no more,
   Not a sigh for the blessing of rest.

3. To our bountiful Father above
   We will offer the tribute of praise.
   For the glorious gift of His love,
   And the blessings that hallow our days.

It Is Well With My Soul

Text by Horatio G. Spafford
Music by Philip P. Bliss

Strum Pattern: 2
Pick Pattern: 2

Additional Lyrics

2. Though Satan should buffet, though trials should come,
   Let this blest assurance control,
   That Christ has regarded my helpless estate,
   And hath shed His own blood for my soul.

3. My sin oh, the bliss of this glorious thought,
   My sin not in part but the whole,
   Is nailed to the cross and I bear it no more,
   Praise the Lord, praise the Lord, oh my soul!

4. And, Lord, haste the day when the faith shall be sight,
   The clouds be rolled back as a scroll,
   The trump shall resound and the Lord shall descend,
   Even so it is well with my soul.

I've Got Peace Like a River

Traditional

Strum Pattern: 3
Pick Pattern: 3

Verse

Joyously

1. I've got peace like a riv - er, I've got peace like a riv - er, I've got

2., 3. *See Additional Lyrics*

peace like a riv - er in my soul. _____ I've got peace like a

riv - er, I've got peace like a riv - er, I've got peace like a

riv - er in ___ my soul. (My soul.) 2. I've got soul. (My soul.)

Additional Lyrics

2. I've got love like an ocean,
   I've got love like an ocean,
   I've got love like an ocean in my soul.
   I've got love like an ocean,
   I've got love like an ocean,
   I've got love like an ocean in my soul. (My soul.)

3. I've got joy like a fountain,
   I've got joy like a fountain,
   I've got joy like a fountain in my soul.
   I've got joy like a fountain,
   I've got joy like a fountain,
   I've got joy like a fountain in my soul. (My soul.)

Jacob's Ladder

African-American Spiritual

Strum Pattern: 8
Pick Pattern: 8

Additional Lyrics

2. Ev'ry rung goes higher, higher.
   Ev'ry rung goes higher, higher.
   Ev'ry rung goes higher, higher.
   Ev'ry rung goes higher, higher.
   Soldiers of the cross.

3. We are climbing higher, higher.
   We are climbing higher, higher.
   We are climbing higher, higher.
   We are climbing higher, higher.
   Soldiers of the cross.

4. If you love Him, why not serve Him?
   If you love Him, why not serve Him?
   If you love Him, why not serve Him?
   If you love Him, why not serve Him?
   Soldiers of the cross.

Jesus Is Tenderly Calling

Words by Fanny J. Crosby
Music by George C. Stebbins

Strum Pattern: 8
Pick Pattern: 8

Verse
Warmly

1. Je - sus is ten - der - ly call - ing thee home, call - ing to - day,
2., 3., 4. *See Additional Lyrics*

call - ing to - day. Why from the sun - shine of love wilt thou roam,

far - ther and far - ther a - way? _____

Chorus

Call - ing to - day, _____ call - ing to - day, _____ Je - sus is

call - ing, is ten - der - ly call - ing to - day. _____ day.

Additional Lyrics

2. Jesus is calling the weary to rest,
   Calling today, calling today.
   Bring Him thy burden and thou shalt be blest;
   He will not turn thee away.

3. Jesus is waiting, O come to Him now,
   Waiting today, waiting today.
   Come with thy sins, at His feet lowly bow;
   Come, and no longer delay.

4. Jesus is pleading, O list to His voice,
   Hear Him today. Hear Him today.
   Those who believe on His name shall rejoice;
   Quickly arise and away.

Jesus, Keep Me Near the Cross

Words by Fanny J. Crosby
Music by William H. Doane

G   Em   C   D   D7

Strum Pattern: 8
Pick Pattern: 8

Verse
Moderately

1. Je - sus, keep me near the cross. There a pre - cious foun - tain,
2., 3., 4. *See Additional Lyrics*

free to all, a heal - ing stream, flows from Cal - v'ry's moun - tain.

Chorus

In the cross, in the cross, be my glo - ry ev - er,

till my rap - tred soul shall find rest be - yond the riv - er. riv - er.

Additional Lyrics

2. Near the cross, a trembling soul,
   Love and mercy found me;
   There the Bright and Morning Star
   Sheds its beams around me.

3. Near the cross! O Lamb of God,
   Bring it scenes before me;
   Help my walk from day to day
   With its shadow's o'er me.

4. Near the cross I'll watch and wait,
   Hoping, trusting ever,
   Till I reach the golden strand
   Just beyond the river.

Jesus, Lover of My Soul

Words by Charles Wesley
Music by Simeon B. Marsh

Strum Pattern: 1, 3
Pick Pattern: 2, 4

Additional Lyrics

2. Other refuge have I none, hangs my helpless soul on Thee;
   Leave, ah! Leave me not alone, still support and comfort me.
   All my trust on Thee is stayed, all my help from Thee I bring;
   Cover my defenseless head with the shadow of the wing.

3. Thou, O Christ, art all I want, more than all in Thee I find;
   Raise the fallen, cheer the faint, heal the sick, and lead the blind.
   Just and holy is Thy name, I am all unrighteousness;
   False and full of sin I am; Thou art full of truth and grace.

4. Plentious grace with Thee is found, grace to cover all my sin;
   Let the healing streams abound, make and keep me pure within.
   Thou of life the fountain art, freely let me take of Thee;
   Spring Thou up within my heart; rise to all eternity.

Jesus Loves Me

Words by Anna Warner
Music by William Bradbury

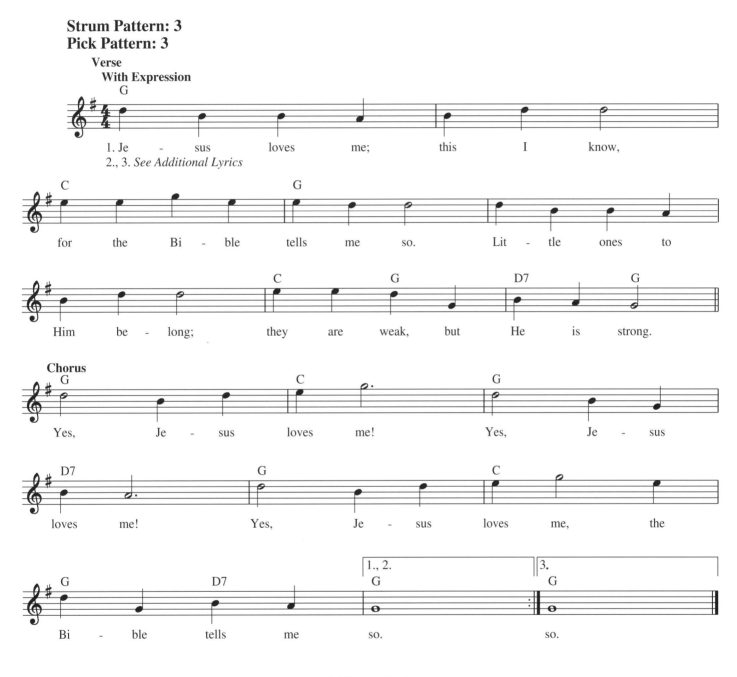

Strum Pattern: 3
Pick Pattern: 3

Verse
With Expression

1. Je - sus loves me; this I know,
2., 3. *See Additional Lyrics*

for the Bi - ble tells me so. Lit - tle ones to

Him be - long; they are weak, but He is strong.

Chorus

Yes, Je - sus loves me! Yes, Je - sus

loves me! Yes, Je - sus loves me, the

Bi - ble tells me so. so.

Additional Lyrics

2. Jesus, take this heart of mine,
   Make it pure and wholly Thine.
   Thou hast bled and died for me,
   I will hence forth live for Thee.

3. Jesus loves me; He who died,
   Heaven's gate to open wide.
   He will wash away my sin,
   Let His little child come in.

Jesus Paid It All

Words and Music by H.M. Hall and John T. Grape

Strum Pattern: 9
Pick Pattern: 7

Additional Lyrics

2. Lord, now indeed I find
   Thy pow'r, and Thine alone
   Can change the leper's spots
   And melt the heart of stone.

3. For nothing good have I
   Whereby Thy grace to claim;
   I'll wash my garments white
   In the blood of Calv'ry's Lamb.

4. And when before the throne
   I stand in Him complete,
   "Jesus died my soul to save,"
   My lips shall still repeat.

Joyful, Joyful We Adore Thee

Words by Henry van Dyke
Music by Ludwig Van Beethoven, melody from Ninth Symphony
Adapted by Edward Hodges

Strum Pattern: 3
Pick Pattern: 4

Verse
Moderately

1. Joy-ful, joy-ful, we a-dore Thee, God of glo-ry, Lord of love;
2., 3. *See Additional Lyrics*

hearts un-fold like flowers be-fore Thee, open-ing to the sun a-bove.

Melt the clouds of sin and __ sad-ness; drive the __ gloom of doubt a-way.

Giv-er of im-mor-tal glad-ness, fill us with the light of day. song of life.

Additional Lyrics

2. All Thy works with joy surround Thee,
   Earth and heaven reflect Thy rays.
   Stars and angels sing around Thee,
   Center of unbroken praise.
   Field and forest, vale and mountain,
   Flowery meadow, flashing sea,
   Chanting bird and flowing fountain,
   Call us to rejoice in Thee.

3. Mortals, join the happy chorus
   Which the morning stars began.
   Love divine is reigning o'er us,
   Joining all in heaven's plan.
   Ever singing, march we onward,
   Victors in the midst of strife.
   Joyful music leads us sunward
   In the triumph song of life.

Just a Closer Walk With Thee

Traditional
Arranged by Kenneth Morris

C   Dm7   G   G7   C7   F#°7

Strum Pattern: 4
Pick Pattern: 1

Verse
Moderately Slow

C ... Dm7 G G7 ... C

1. I am weak but Thou art strong; Je - sus, keep me from all wrong. ____
2., 3. *See Additional Lyrics*

C7 ... Dm7 F#°7 C G7 C

I'll be sat - is - fied as long ____ as I walk, let me walk close to Thee.

Chorus

C ... Dm7 G G7 ... C

Just a clos - er walk with Thee, grant it, Je - sus, is my plea. ____

C7 ... Dm7 F#°7 C G7 1., 2. C | 3. C

Dai - ly walk-ing close to Thee, ____ let it be, dear Lord, let it be. be.

Additional Lyrics

2. Through this world of toil and snares,
   If I falter, Lord, who cares?
   Who with me my burden shares?
   None but Thee, dear Lord, none but Thee.

3. When my feeble life is o'er,
   Time for me will be no more;
   Guide me gently, safely o'er
   To Thy kingdom shore, to Thy shore.

Just As I Am

Words by Charlotte Elliott
Music by William Bradbury

Strum Pattern: 7, 8
Pick Pattern: 7, 8

Verse
Moderately Slow

1. Just as I am, with- out one plea but

2. – 5. *See Additional Lyrics*

that Thy blood was shed for me, and that Thou

bidd'st me come to Thee, O Lamb of God, I

come! I come! 2. Just come!

Additional Lyrics

2. Just as I am, and waiting not
   To rid my soul of one dark blot,
   To Thee whose blood can cleanse each spot,
   O Lamb of God, I come! I come!

3. Just as I am, though tossed about
   With many a conflict, many a doubt,
   Fightings and fears within, without,
   O Lamb of God, I come! I come!

4. Just as I am, poor, wretched, blind
   Sight, riches, healing of the mind.
   Yeah, all I need in Thee to find
   O Lamb of God, I come! I come!

5. Just as I am, Thou wilt receive,
   Wilt welcome, pardon, cleanse, relieve;
   Because Thy promise I believe,
   O Lamb of God, I come! I come!

Leaning on the Everlasting Arms

Words by Elisha A. Hoffman
Music by Anthony J. Showalter

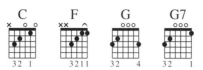

Strum Pattern: 4, 5
Pick Pattern: 1, 3

Additional Lyrics

2. Oh, how sweet to walk in this pilgrim way,
   Leaning on the everlasting arms.
   Oh, how bright the path grows from day to day.
   Leaning on the everlasting arms.

Let Us Break Bread Together

African-American Spiritual

Strum Pattern: 3
Pick Pattern: 3

Verse
Moderately

1. Let us break bread to-geth-er on our knees, (On our knees.) let us
2., 3. *See Additional Lyrics*

break bread to-geth-er on our knees. (On our knees.) When I

Chorus

fall on my knees with my face to the ris-ing sun, oh

Lord, have mer-cy on me. (On me.) 2. Let us me.)

Additional Lyrics

2. Let us drink the cup together on our knees.
   (On our knees.)
   Let us drink the cup together on our knees.
   (On our knees.)

3. Let us praise God together on our knees.
   (On our knees.)
   Let us praise God together on our knees.
   (On our knees.)

Like a River Glorious

Words by Frances Ridley Havergal
Music by James Mountain

Strum Pattern: 4
Pick Pattern: 4

Like a riv-er glo-rious is God's per-fect peace,

o-ver all vic-to-rious in its bright in-crease.

Per-fect, yet it flow-eth, full-er ev-'ry day.

Per-fect, yet it grow-eth, deep-er all the way. true.

Additional Lyrics

2. Hidden in the hollow of His blessed hand,
   Never foe can follow, never traitor stand.
   Not a surge of worry, not a shade of care,
   Not a blast of hurry touch the Spirit there.

3. Ev'ry joy or trial falleth from above,
   Traced upon our dial by the sun of love.
   We must trust him fully, all for us to do.
   They who trust Him wholly find Him wholly true.

The Lily of the Valley

Words by Charles W. Fry
Music by William S. Hays

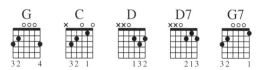

Strum Pattern: 3, 4
Pick Pattern: 1, 3

Additional Lyrics

2. He all my grief has taken, and all my sorrows borne.
   In temptation He's my strong and mighty tower;
   I have all for Him forsaken, all my idols torn.
   From my heart, and now He keeps me by His power.
   Though all the world forsake me,
   And Satan tempt me sore,
   Through Jesus I shall safely reach the goal.

3. He will never, never leave me, nor yet forsake me here,
   While I live by faith and do His blessed will.
   A wall of fire about me, I've nothing now to fear,
   With His manna He my hungry soul shall fill.
   Then sweeping up to glory
   To see His blessed face,
   Where rivers of delight shall ever roll.

Lord, I Want to Be a Christian

Traditional Negro Spiritual

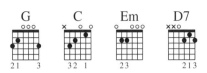

Strum Pattern: 1, 3
Pick Pattern: 2, 4

Additional Lyrics

2. Lord, I want to be more loving in my heart, in my heart;
   Lord, I want to be more loving in my heart. (In my heart.)
   In my heart, in my heart,
   Lord, I want to be more loving in my heart.

3. Lord, I want to be more holy in my heart, in my heart;
   Lord, I want to be more holy in my heart. (In my heart.)
   In my heart, in my heart,
   Lord, I want to be more holy in my heart.

4. Lord, I want to be like Jesus in my heart, in my heart;
   Lord, I want to be like Jesus in my heart. (In my heart.)
   In my heart, in my heart.
   Lord, I want to be like Jesus in my heart.

Love Divine, All Loves Excelling

Words by Charles Wesley
Music by John Zundel

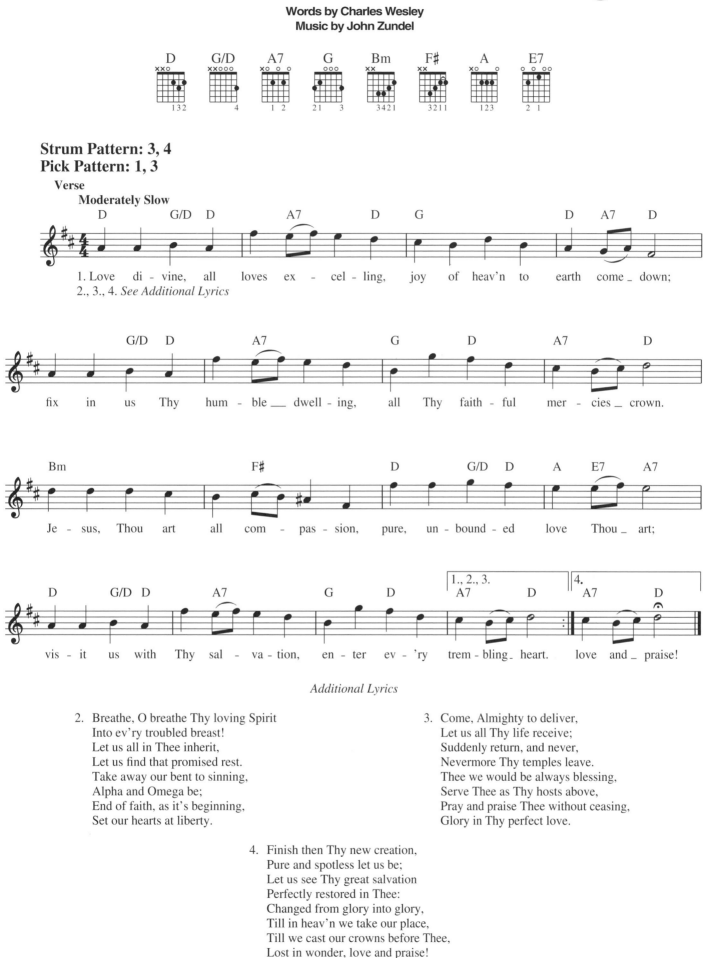

Additional Lyrics

2. Breathe, O breathe Thy loving Spirit
   Into ev'ry troubled breast!
   Let us all in Thee inherit,
   Let us find that promised rest.
   Take away our bent to sinning,
   Alpha and Omega be;
   End of faith, as it's beginning,
   Set our hearts at liberty.

3. Come, Almighty to deliver,
   Let us all Thy life receive;
   Suddenly return, and never,
   Nevermore Thy temples leave.
   Thee we would be always blessing,
   Serve Thee as Thy hosts above,
   Pray and praise Thee without ceasing,
   Glory in Thy perfect love.

4. Finish then Thy new creation,
   Pure and spotless let us be;
   Let us see Thy great salvation
   Perfectly restored in Thee:
   Changed from glory into glory,
   Till in heav'n we take our place,
   Till we cast our crowns before Thee,
   Lost in wonder, love and praise!

Love Lifted Me

Words and Music by James Rowe and Howard E. Smith

Strum Pattern: 8
Pick Pattern: 8

Verse
Moderately Fast

1. I was sinking deep in sin, far from the peaceful shore, very deeply
2., 3. *See Additional Lyrics*

stained within, sinking to rise no more. But the Master of the sea

heard my despairing cry, from the waters lifted me; now safe am I.

Chorus

Love lifted me! Love lifted me! When nothing else could help,

love lifted me. Love lifted me! Love lifted me!

When nothing else could help, love lifted me. me. _____

Additional Lyrics

2. All my heart to Him I give, ever to Him I'll cling,
In His blessed presence live, ever His praises sing;
Love so mighty and so true merits my soul's best songs;
Faithful, loving service, too to Him belongs.

3. Souls in danger, look above Jesus completely saves,
He will lift you by His love out of the angry waves;
He's the Master of the sea, billows His will obey;
He your Savior wants to be, be saved today.

A Mighty Fortress Is Our God

Words and Music by Martin Luther

Strum Pattern: 1, 6
Pick Pattern: 2, 4

*Combine Patterns 8 & 10   **Combine Patterns 1 & 10

1. A might-y for-tress is __ our God, a bul-wark nev-er fail-
2., 3., 4. *See Additional Lyrics*

ing; our Help-er He __ a - mid __ the flood of mor-tal ills pre-vail-

ing. For still our an - cient foe doth seek to work us

woe. His craft and pow'r are great, and armed with cru - el

hate, on earth is not his e - qual. 2. Did er.

Additional Lyrics

2. Did we in our own strength confide,
Our striving would be losing,
Were not the right man on our side,
The man of God's own choosing.
Dost ask who that may be?
Christ Jesus, it is He.
Lord Sabaoth His name,
From age to age the same,
And He must win the battle.

3. And though this world, with devils filled,
Should threaten to undo us,
We will not fear, for God has willed
His truth to triumph through us.
The prince of darkness grim,
We tremble not for him.
His rage we can endure,
For lo, his doom is sure:
One little word shall fell him.

4. That word above all earthly pow'rs,
No thanks to men, abideth;
The Spirit and the gifts are ours
Through Him who with us sideth.
Let goods and kindred go,
This mortal life also.
The body they may kill:
God's truth abideth still:
His kingdom is forever.

Mine Eyes Have Seen the Glory

Words by Julia Ward Howe
Music by William Steffe

Strum Pattern: 4
Pick Pattern: 1

Additional Lyrics

2. I have seen Him in the watchfires of a hundred circling camps,
   They have builded Him an altar in the evening dews and damps.
   I can read His righteous sentence by the dim and flaring lamps,
   His day is marching on.

3. He has sounded forth the trumpet that shall never call retreat,
   He is sifting out the hearts of men before His judgment seat.
   Oh, be swift, my soul, to answer Him, be jubilant, my feet,
   Our God is marching on.

My Faith Has Found a Resting Place

Words by Lidie H. Edmunds
Music by Andre Gretry

Strum Pattern: 8
Pick Pattern: 8

Verse
Moderately

1. My faith has found a rest-ing place, not in a man-made creed. I
2., 3., 4. *See Additional Lyrics*

trust the ev - er liv - ing One, that He for me will plead. I

Chorus

need no oth - er ar - gu - ment, I need no oth - er plea, _____ it

is e - nough that Je - sus died and rose a - gain for me. 2. E - me.

Additional Lyrics

2. Enough for me that Jesus saves,
   This ends my fear and doubt.
   A sinful soul I come to Him,
   He will not cast me out.

3. My soul is resting on the Word,
   The living Word of God.
   Salvation in my Savior's name,
   Salvation through His blood.

4. The great Physician heals the sick,
   The lost He came to save;
   For me His precious blood He shed,
   For me His life He gave.

My Jesus, I Love Thee

Text by William R. Featherstone
Music by Adoniram J. Gordon

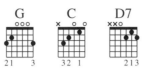

Strum Pattern: 3
Pick Pattern: 3

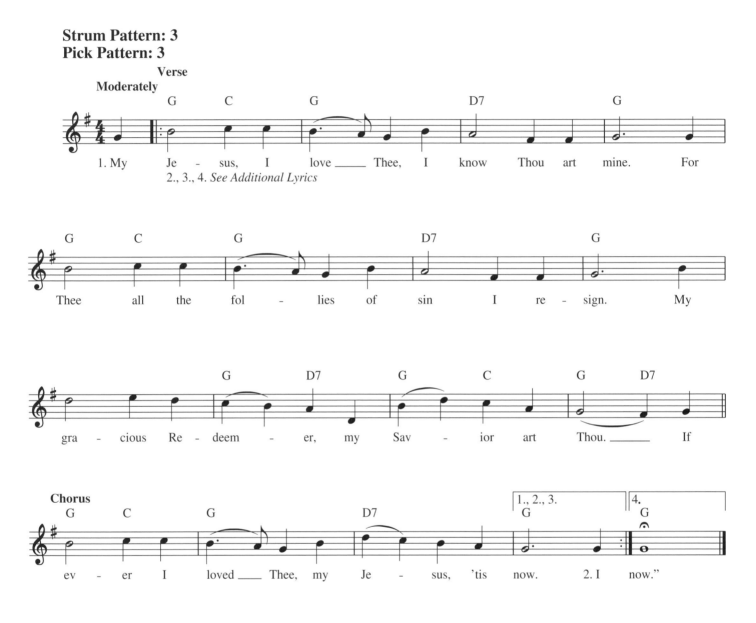

Additional Lyrics

2. I love Thee because Thou hast first loved me
   And purchased my pardon on Calvary's tree.
   I love Thee for wearing the thorns on Thy brow.

3. I'll love Thee in life, I will love Thee in death,
   And praise Thee as long as Thou lendest me breath.
   And say when the death dew lies cold on my brow, "If…

4. In mansions of glory and endless delight,
   I'll ever adore Thee in heaven so bright.
   I'll sing with the glittering crown on my brow, "If…

My Savior First of All

Words by Fanny J. Crosby
Music by John R. Sweney

Strum Pattern: 1, 3
Pick Pattern: 4, 6

Verse
Moderately Slow

1. When my life - work is end - ed and I cross the swell - ing tide, when the
2., 3., 4. *See Additional Lyrics*

bright and glo - rious morn - ing I shall see; I shall know my Re - deem - er when I

reach the oth - er side, and His smile will be the first to wel - come me. I shall

Chorus

know _____ Him, I shall know Him, and re - deemed by His side _ I shall stand; I shall

know _____ Him, I shall know Him by the prints of the nails _ in His hand. 2. O the hand.

Additional Lyrics

2. O the soul thrilling rapture when I view His blessed face
   And the luster of His kindly beaming eye;
   How my full heart will praise Him for the mercy, love and grace
   That prepare for me a mansion in the sky.

3. O the dear ones in glory, how They beckon me to come,
   And our parting at the river I recall;
   To the sweet vales of Eden They will sing my welcome home,
   But I long to meet my Savior first of all.

4. Through the gates to the city in a robe of spotless white,
   He will lead me where no tears will ever fall
   In the glad song of ages I shall mingle with delight,
   But I long to meet my Savior first of all.

My Savior's Love

Words and Music by Charles H. Gabriel

Strum Pattern: 4
Pick Pattern: 1

Verse
Moderately

1. I stand a-mazed in the pres-ence of Je-sus, the Naz-a-rene, and
2. – 5. *See Additional Lyrics*

won-der how He could love me, a sin-ner, con-demned, un-clean.

Chorus

How mar-vel-ous, how won-der-ful! And my song shall ev-er be:
(O how mar-vel-ous, O how won-der-ful!)

How mar-vel-ous, how won-der-ful! Is my _ Sav-ior's love for me! 2. For love for me!
(O how mar-vel-ous, O how won-der-ful!)

Additional Lyrics

2. For me it was in the garden
   He prayed, "Not My will, but Thine."
   He had no tears for His own griefs,
   But sweat drops of blood for mine.

3. In pity angels beheld Him
   And came from the world of light
   To comfort Him in the sorrows
   He bore for my soul that night.

4. He took my sins and my sorrows;
   He made them His very own.
   He bore the burden to Calv'ry
   And suffered and died alone.

5. When with the ransomed in glory
   His face I at last shall see,
   'Twill be my joy through the ages
   To sing of His love for me.

Near the Cross

Words by Fanny Crosby
Music by William H. Doane

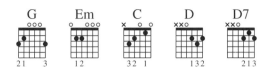

Strum Pattern: 8
Pick Pattern: 8

Additional Lyrics

2. Near the cross, a trembling soul,
Love and mercy found me.
There the bright and morning star
Sheds its beams around me.

3. Near the cross! Oh Lamb of God,
Bring its scenes before me.
Help my walk from day to day,
With its shadows o'er me.

4. Near the cross I'll watch and wait,
Hoping, trusting ever,
Till I reach the golden strand
Just beyond the river.

Near to the Heart of God

Traditional Text by Cleland B. McAfee
Traditional Music

Strum Pattern: 1, 3
Pick Pattern: 2, 4

Verse
Moderately Slow

1. There is a place of qui - et rest, near to the heart of God; a
2., 3. *See Additional Lyrics*

place where sin can - not mo - lest, near to the heart of God. O

Chorus

Je - sus, blest Re - deem - er, sent from the heart of God, hold

us, who wait be - fore Thee, near to the heart of God. 2. There God.

Additional Lyrics

2. There is a place of comfort sweet,
   Near to the heart of God;
   A place where we our Savior meet,
   Near to the heart of God.

3. There is a place of full release,
   Near to the heart of God;
   A place where all is joy and peace,
   Near to the heart of God.

Nearer My God to Thee

Text by Sarah F. Adams
Music by Lowell Mason

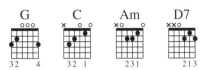

Strum Pattern: 4, 5
Pick Pattern: 1, 3

Verse

Moderately

1. Near - er, my God, to Thee, near - er to Thee!
2., 3., 4. *See Additional Lyrics*

E'en though it be a cross that _____ rais - eth me.

Still all my song shall be, near - er, my God, to Thee.

Near - er, my God, to Thee, near - er to Thee! Thee!

Additional Lyrics

2. Though, like the wanderer,
The sun gone down,
Darkness be over me
My rest a stone.
Yet in my dreams I'd be,
Nearer, my God, to Thee.
Nearer, my God, to Thee,
Nearer to Thee!

3. Then with my waking thoughts
Bright with Thy praise,
Out of my stony griefs
Bethel I'll raise.
So by my woes to be,
Nearer, my God, to Thee.
Nearer, my God, to Thee,
Nearer to Thee!

4. Or if on joyful wing,
Cleaving the sky,
Sun, moon and stars forgot,
Upwards I'll fly.
Still all my song shall be,
Nearer, my God, to Thee.
Nearer, my God, to Thee,
Nearer to Thee!

Nothing But the Blood

Words and Music by Robert Lowry

Strum Pattern: 4
Pick Pattern: 1

Verse
Moderately Slow

1. What can wash a - way my sin? Noth-ing but the blood of Je - sus;
2., 3., 4. *See Additional Lyrics*

what can make me whole a - gain? Noth-ing but the blood of Je - sus.

Chorus

O pre - cious is the flow that makes me white as snow; ___

no oth - er fount I know, noth-ing but the blood of Je - sus. Je - sus.

Additional Lyrics

2. For my pardon this I see,
   Nothing but the blood of Jesus;
   For my cleansing, this my plea,
   Nothing but the blood of Jesus.

3. Nothing can for sin atone,
   Nothing but the blood of Jesus;
   Naught of good that I have done,
   Nothing but the blood of Jesus.

4. This is all my hope and peace,
   Nothing but the blood of Jesus;
   This is all my righteousness,
   Nothing but the blood of Jesus.

Now Thank We All Our God

German Words by Martin Rinkart
English Translation by Catherine Winkworth
Music by Johann Crüger

G   C   Am   D7   A   D   Em   E

Strum Pattern: 3
Pick Pattern: 4

Verse
Moderately

G   C   G   Am   D7   G

1. Now thank we all our God with heart and hands and voi - ces, who
2., 3. *See Additional Lyrics*

C   G   Am   D7   G

won - drous things have done in whom His world re - joi - ces. Who

A   G   D   G   Em   D

from our moth - er's arms hath blest __ us on our way, with

E   Am   D7   1., 2. G   3. G

count - less gifts of love, and still is ours to - day. 2. Oh more.

Additional Lyrics

2. Oh may this bounteous God through all our life be near us,
   With ever joyful hearts and blessed peace to cheer us.
   And keep us in His grace and guide us when perplexed,
   And free us from all ills in this world and the next.

3. All praise and thanks to God, the Father now be given,
   The Son and Him who reigns with them in highest heaven.
   The one eternal God, whom earth and heaven adore,
   For thus it was, is now and shall be evermore.

O For a Thousand Tongues to Sing

Text by Charles Wesley
Music by Carl G. Glaser

Strum Pattern: 8
Pick Pattern: 8

Verse
Moderately Slow

1. O for a thou-sand tongues to sing my great Re-deem-er's praise; the
2. – 5. *See Additional Lyrics*

glo-ries of my God and King, the ___ tri-umphs of His grace! 2. My joy!

Additional Lyrics

2. My gracious Master and my God,
   Assist me to proclaim,
   To spread through all the earth abroad
   The honors of Thy name.

3. Jesus! The name that charms our fears,
   That bids our sorrows cease,
   'Tis music in the sinner's ears,
   'Tis life and health and peace.

4. He breaks the pow'r of canceled sin,
   He sets the prisoner free;
   His blood can make the foulest clean,
   His blood availed for me.

5. Hear Him, ye deaf, His praise, ye dumb,
   Your loosened tongues employ;
   Ye blind, behold your Savior come,
   And leap, ye lame, for joy!

O God Our Help in Ages Past

Words by Isaac Watts
Music by St. Anne
Melody attributed to William Croft

Strum Pattern: 4
Pick Pattern: 3

Additional Lyrics

2. A thousand ages, in Thy sight, are like an evening gone;
Short as the watch that ends the night, before the rising sun.
Time, like an ever rolling stream, bears all who breathe away;
They fly forgotten, as a dream dies at the opening day.
O God, our help in ages past, our hope for years to come.
Be Thou our guide while life shall last, and our eternal home.

O Happy Day

Words by Philip Doddridge
Music from William McDonald's Wesleyan Sacred Harp

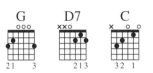

Strum Pattern: 8
Pick Pattern: 8

Additional Lyrics

2. O happy bond, that seals my vows
   To Him who merits all my love!
   Let cheerful anthems fill His house,
   While to that sacred shrine I move.

3. 'Tis done, the great transaction's done;
   I am my Lord's and He is mine;
   He drew me and I followed on,
   Rejoiced to own the call divine.

4. Now rest, my long-divided heart,
   Fixed on this blissful center, rest;
   Here have I found a nobler part,
   Here heavenly pleasures fill my breast.

5. High heaven that hears the solemn vow,
   That vow renewed shall daily hear;
   Till in life's latest hour I bow,
   And bless, in death, a bond so dear.

O Love That Wilt Not Let Me Go

Words by George Matheson
Music by Albert Lister Peace

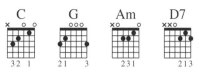

Strum Pattern: 3
Pick Pattern: 4

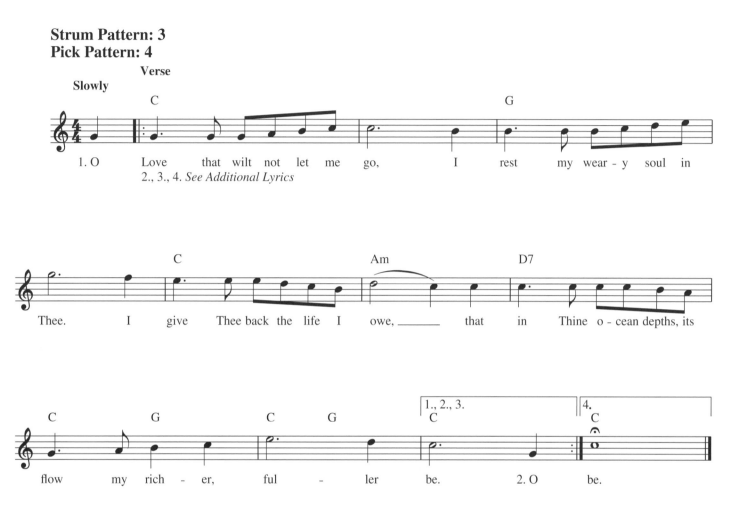

Additional Lyrics

2. O light that foll'west all my way,
   I yield my flick'ring torch to Thee.
   My heart restores its borrowed ray,
   That in Thy sunshine's glow its day
   May brighter, fairer be.

3. O joy that seekest me through pain,
   I cannot close my heart to Thee.
   I trace the rainbow through the rain,
   And feel the promise is not vain.
   That morn shall tearless be.

4. O cross that liftest up my head,
   I dare not ask to hide from Thee.
   I lay in dust, life's glory dead,
   And from the ground there, blossoms red,
   Life that shall endless be.

O Perfect Love

Words by Dorothy Frances Gurney
Music by Joseph Barnby

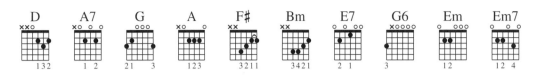

Strum Pattern: 1, 2
Pick Pattern: 4, 5

Verse
Tenderly

1. O per - fect love, all hu - man thought tran - scend - ing,
2., 3. *See Additional Lyrics*

low - ly we kneel in prayer be - fore Thy throne,

That theirs may be the love which knows no end - ing,

1., 2.
whom Thou for - ev - er - more dost join in one.

3.
that dawns up - on e - ter - nal love and life. _____

Additional Lyrics

2. O perfect life, be Thou their full assurance
   Of tender charity and steadfast faith,
   Of patient hope and quiet, brave endurance,
   With child-like trust that fears no pain nor death.

3. Grant them the joy which brightens earthly sorrow,
   Grant them the peace which calms all earthly strife,
   And to life's day the glorious unknown morrow
   That dawns upon eternal love and life.

Oh, How I Love Jesus

Words by Frederick Whitfield
Traditional American Melody

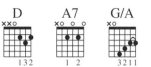

Strum Pattern: 8
Pick Pattern: 8

Additional Lyrics

2. It tells me of a Savior's love,
   Who died to set me free;
   It tells me of His precious blood,
   The sinner's perfect plea.

3. It tells me what my Father hath
   In store for ev'ry day;
   And though I tread a darksome path,
   Yields sunshine all the way.

4. It tells of One whose loving heart
   Can feel my deepest woe,
   Who in each sorrow bears a part
   That none can bear below.

The Old Rugged Cross

Words and Music by Rev. George Bennard

Strum Pattern: 8
Pick Pattern: 8

Additonal Lyrics

2. To the old rugged cross I will ever be true,
   Its shame and reproach gladly bear;
   Then He'll call me some day to my home far away,
   Where His glory forever I'll share.

On Jordan's Stormy Banks

Words by Samuel Stennett
American Folk Hymn Arranged by Rigdon M. McIntosh

Strum Pattern: 3
Pick Pattern: 3

Additional Lyrics

2. All o'er these wide extended plains
   Shines one eternal day.
   There God the Son forever reigns
   And scatters night away.

3. No chilling winds nor pois'nous breath
   Can reach that healthful shore;
   Sickness and sorrow, pain and death
   Are felt and feared no more.

4. When shall I reach that happy place
   And be forever blest?
   When shall I see my Father's face
   And in His bosom rest?

Once to Every Man and Nation

Words by James Russel Lowell
Music by Thomas J. Williams

Em   B7   C   G   D   Am   Dsus4

Strum Pattern: 4
Pick Pattern: 1

Verse
Stately

1. Once to ____ ev - 'ry man and ____ na - tion comes the ____ mo - ment
2., 3. *See Additional Lyrics*

to ____ de - cide, in the ____ strife of truth with ____ false - hood,

for the ____ good ____ or e - vil side; some great ____ cause, some

great de - ci - sion, of - f'ring ____ each the bloom or ____ blight, and the ____ choice goes

by for - ev - er 'twixt that ____ dark - ness and __ that light. bove _ His own.

Additional Lyrics

2. Then to side with truth is noble,
When we share her wretched crust,
Ere her cause bring fame and profit,
And 'tis prosp'rous to be just;
Then it is the brave man chooses
While the coward stands aside,
Till the multitude make virtue
Of the faith they had denied.

3. Though the cause of evil prosper,
Yet the truth alone is strong;
Though her portion be the scaffold,
And upon the throne be wrong,
Yet that scaffold sways the future,
And behind the dim unknown,
Standeth God within the shadow,
Keeping watch above His own.

Only Trust Him

Words and Music by John H. Stockton

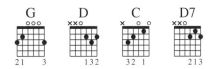

Strum Pattern: 4, 5
Pick Pattern: 1, 3

Additional Lyrics

2. For Jesus shed His precious blood,
   Rich blessings to bestow;
   Plunge now into the crimson flood
   That washes white as snow.

3. Yes, Jesus is the truth, the way,
   That leads you into rest;
   Believe in Him without delay,
   And you are fully blest.

4. Come, then, and join this holy band,
   And on to glory go,
   To dwell in that celestial land,
   Where joys immortal flow.

Onward Christian Soldiers

Words by Sabine Baring-Gould
Music by Arthur S. Sullivan

Strum Pattern: 4, 5
Pick Pattern: 1, 3

Additional Lyrics

2. Like a mighty army moves the Church of God.
   Brothers we are treading where the saints have trod.
   We are not divided, all one body we.
   One in hope and doctrine, one in charity.

3. Onward, then, ye people join our happy throng.
   Blend with ours your voices in the triumph song.
   Glory, laud, and honor unto Christ the King.
   This through countless ages men and angels sing.

Open My Eyes, That I May See

Words and Music by Clara H. Scott

Strum Pattern: 8
Pick Pattern: 8

Verse
Moderately

1. O - pen my eyes, that I may see glimps - es of truth Thou hast for me;
2., 3. *See Additional Lyrics*

place in my hands the won - der - ful key that shall un - clasp and set me free.

Chorus

Si - lent - ly now I wait for Thee. Read - y my God, Thy will to see; o - pen my { eyes, ears, heart, } il -

lu - mine me, Spir - it di - vine! vine! ____

Additional Lyrics

2. Open my ears, that I may hear
   Voices of truth Thou sendest clear;
   And while the wave notes fall on my ear,
   Ev'rything false will disappear.

3. Open my mouth, and let me bear
   Gladly the warm truth ev'rywhere;
   Open my heart, and let me prepare
   Love with Thy children thus to share.

Our Great Savior

Words by J. Wilbur Chapman
Music by Rowland H. Prichard

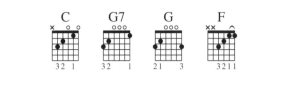

Strum Pattern: 8
Pick Pattern: 8

Verse
Moderately

1. Je - sus! What ___ a Friend for sin - ners! Je - sus!
2. – 5. *See Additional Lyrics*

Lov - er of ___ my soul; friends may fail ___ me, foes as -

sail ___ me, He, my Sav - ior, makes ___ me whole.

Chorus

Hal - le - lu - jah! What a Sav - ior! Hal - le - lu - jah!

What ___ a Friend! Sav - ing, help - ing, keep - ing lov - ing,

He is with ___ me to the end. end. ___

Additional Lyrics

2. Jesus! What a strength in weakness!
   Let me hide myself in Him;
   Tempted, tried, and sometimes failing,
   He, my strength, my vict'ry wins.

3. Jesus! What a help in sorrow!
   While the billows o'er me roll,
   Even when my heart is breaking,
   He, my comfort, helps my soul.

4. Jesus! What a Guide and Keeper!
   While the tempest still is high,
   Storms about me, night o'ertakes me,
   He, my Pilot, hears my cry.

5. Jesus! I do now receive Him,
   More than all in Him I find;
   He hath granted me forgiveness,
   I am His, and He is mine.

Pass Me Not, O Gentle Savior

Words by Fanny J. Crosby
Music by William H. Doane

G   C   D   D7

Strum Pattern: 5
Pick Pattern: 1

Verse
Moderately

1. Pass me not, oh gen - tle Sav - ior, hear my hum - ble cry!
2., 3., 4. *See Additional Lyrics*

While on oth - ers Thou art call - ing, do not pass me by.

Chorus

Sav - ior, Sav - ior, hear my hum - ble cry!

1., 2., 3. | *4.*

While on oth - ers Thou art call - ing, do not pass me by. by.

Additional Lyrics

2. Let me at a throne of mercy,
   Find a sweet relief;
   Kneeling there in deep contrition
   Help my unbelief.

3. Trusting only in Thy merit,
   Would I seek Thy face;
   Heal my wounded, broken spirit,
   Save me by Thy grace.

4. Thou the spring of all my comfort,
   More than life to me!
   Whom have I on earth beside Thee?
   Whom in heav'n but Thee!

Praise God, From Whom All Blessings Flow

Words by Thomas Ken
Music Attributed to Louis Bourgeois

Rise Up, O Men of God

Words by William Pierson Merrill
Music by William H. Walter

Additional Lyrics

2. Rise up, O men of God!
   His kingdom tarries long;
   Bring in the day of brotherhood
   And end the night of wrong.

3. Rise up, O men of God!
   How long the church must wait,
   Her strength unequal to her task.
   Rise up, and make her great!

4. Lift high the cross of Christ!
   Tread where His feet have trod;
   As brothers of the Son of Man,
   Rise up, O men of God!

Praise Him, Praise Him

Words and Music by Fanny Crosby and Chester Allen

Strum Pattern: 8
Pick Pattern: 8

Additional Lyrics

2. Praise Him! Praise Him! Jesus our blessed Redeemer!
   For our sins He suffered, and bled, and died.
   He our Rock, our Hope of eternal salvation.
   Hail Him! Hail Him! Jesus the Crucified.
   Sound His praises! Jesus who bore our sorrows;
   Love unbounded, wonderful, deep and strong!

3. Praise Him! Praise Him! Jesus, our blessed Redeemer!
   Heav'nly portals loud with hosannas ring!
   Jesus, Savior, reigneth forever and ever.
   Crown Him! Crown Him! Prophet, and Priest, and King!
   Christ is coming, over the world victorious;
   Pow'r and glory unto the Lord belong!

Rejoice, the Lord Is King

Words by Charles Wesley
Music by John Darwall

Strum Pattern: 4
Pick Pattern: 1

Verse
Moderately Slow

1. Re - joice, the Lord is King! Your Lord and King a -
2., 3. *See Additional Lyrics*

dore! Re - joice, give thanks, and sing, and tri - umph ev - er -

Chorus

more. Lift up your heart, lift up your voice! Re -

joice, a - gain I say, re - joice! 2. God's joice!

Additional Lyrics

2. God's kingdom cannot fail,
   Christ rules o'er earth and heaven;
   The keys of death and hell
   Are to our Jesus given.

3. Rejoice in glorious hope!
   For Christ, the Judge, shall come
   To glorify the saints
   For their eternal home.

Rescue the Perishing

Words by Fanny J. Crosby
Music by William H. Doane

Strum Pattern: 4
Pick Pattern: 1

Additional Lyrics

2. Though they are slighting Him, still He is waiting,
   Waiting the penitent child to receive;
   Plead with them earnestly, plead with them gently,
   He will forgive if they only believe.

3. Down in the human heart, crushed by the tempter,
   Feelings lie buried that grace can restore;
   Touched by a loving heart, wakened by kindness,
   Cords that are broken will vibrate once more.

4. Rescue the perishing, duty demands it
   Strength for our labor the Lord will provide;
   Back to the narrow way patiently win them,
   Tell the poor wand'rer a Savior has died.

Ring the Bells of Heaven

Traditional

Strum Pattern: 4
Pick Pattern: 1

Verse
Moderately Slow

1. Ring the bells of heav - en! There is joy to-day, for a soul, re-turn - ing from the wild!
2., 3. *See Additional Lyrics*

See, the Fa - ther meets him out up-on the way, wel - com-ing His wear - y, wan - d'ring child.

Chorus

Glo - ry! Glo - ry! How the an - gels sing; glo - ry! Glo - ry! How the loud harps ring! loud harps ring!

Outro

'Tis the ran - somed ar - my, like a might - y sea, peal - ing forth the an - them of the free.

Additional Lyrics

2. Ring the bells of heaven!
   There is joy today,
   For the wand'rer now is reconciled;
   Yes, a soul is rescued
   From his sinful way,
   And is born anew a ransomed child.

3. Ring the bells of heaven!
   Spread the feat today!
   Angels swell the glad triumphant strain!
   Tell the joyful tidins,
   Bear it far away!
   For a precious soul is born again.

Savior Like a Shepherd Lead Us

Words attributed to Dorothy A. Thrupp
Music by William B. Bradbury

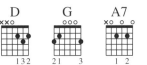

Strum Pattern: 2
Pick Pattern: 2

1. Sav - ior, like a shep-herd lead ___ us, ___ much we need Thy ten-d'rest care.
2., 3., 4. *See Additional Lyrics*

In Thy pleas-ant pas-tures feed ___ us, ___ for our use Thy folds pre - pare. Bless-sed

Je - sus, bless-ed Je - sus, Thou hast bought us, Thine we are. Bless-ed

Je - sus, bless-ed Je - sus, Thou hast bought us, Thine we are. still.

Additional Lyrics

2. We are Thine; do Thou befriend us,
   Be the Guardian of our way.
   Keep Thy flock, from sin defend us,
   Seek us when we go astray.
   Blessed Jesus, blessed Jesus,
   Hear, oh hear us when we pray;
   Blessed Jesus, blessed Jesus,
   Hear, oh hear us when we pray.

3. Thou hast promised to receive us,
   Poor and sinful though we be.
   Thou hast mercy to relieve us,
   Grace to cleanse, and pow'r to free.
   Blessed Jesus, blessed Jesus,
   Early let us turn to Thee.
   Blessed Jesus, blessed Jesus,
   Early let us turn to Thee.

4. Early let us seek Thy favor,
   Early let us do Thy will.
   Blessed Lord and only Savior,
   With Thy love our bosoms fill.
   Blessed Jesus, blessed Jesus,
   Thou hast loved us, love us still.
   Blessed Jesus, blessed Jesus,
   Thou hast loved us, love us still.

Rock of Ages

Text by Augstus M. Toplady
Music by Thomas Hastings

Strum Pattern: 8
Pick Pattern: 8

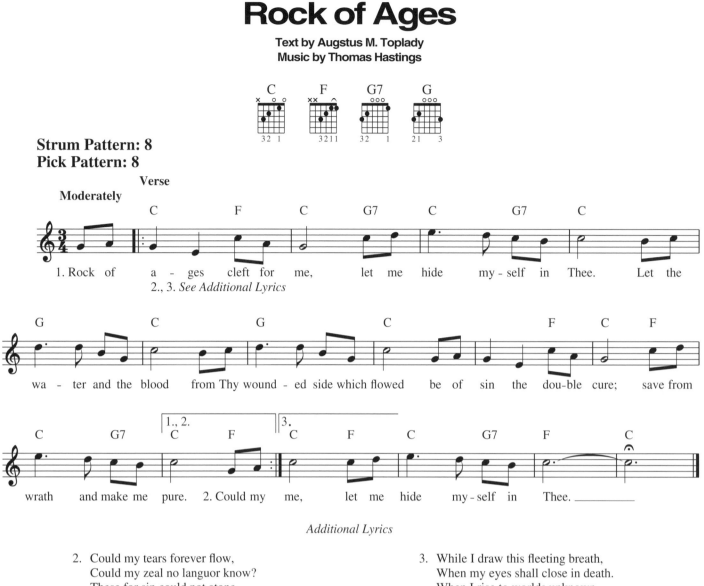

1. Rock of a-ges cleft for me, let me hide my-self in Thee. Let the
2., 3. *See Additional Lyrics*

wa-ter and the blood from Thy wound-ed side which flowed be of sin the dou-ble cure; save from

wrath and make me pure. 2. Could my me, let me hide my-self in Thee._____

Additional Lyrics

2. Could my tears forever flow,
Could my zeal no languor know?
These for sin could not atone,
Thou must save and Thou alone.
I my hand no price I bring,
Simply to Thy cross I cling.

3. While I draw this fleeting breath,
When my eyes shall close in death.
When I rise to worlds unknown,
And behold Thee on Thy throne.
Rock of ages cleft for me,
Let me hide myself in Thee,
Let me hide myself in Thee.

Whispering Hope

Words and Music by Alice Hawthorne

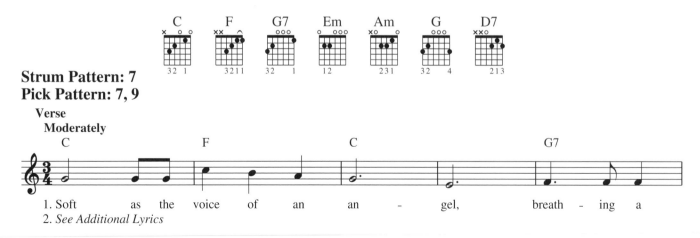

Strum Pattern: 7
Pick Pattern: 7, 9

Verse
Moderately

1. Soft as the voice of an an-gel, breath-ing a
2. *See Additional Lyrics*

les - son un - heard. _____ Hope with a gen - tle per - sua -

sion, whis - pers her com - fort - ing word. _____ Wait till the

dark - ness is o - ver, wait till the tem - pest is done. _____

Hope for the sun - shine to - mor - row, af - ter the show - er is

Chorus

gone. _____ Whis - per - ing hope. _____ Oh, how

wel - come thy voice. _____ Mak - ing my

1.
heart _____ in the sor - row re - joice. _____

2.
heart _____ in the sor - row re - joice. _____

Additional Lyrics

2. If in the dusk of the twilight,
   Dim be the region afar.
   Will not the deepening darkness
   Brighten the glimmering star?
   Then when the night is upon us,
   Why should the heart sink away?
   When the dark midnight is over,
   Watch for the breaking of day.

Send the Light

Words and Music by Charles Gabriel

Strum Pattern: 4
Pick Pattern: 1

Verse
Moderately Slow

1. There's a call come ring-ing o'er the rest-less wave, "Send the light! Send the light!" There are
2., 3., 4. *See Additional Lyrics*

souls to res-cue; there are souls to save. Send the light! Send the light! Send the

Chorus

light, _____ the bless-ed gos-pel light; let it shine _____ from shore to shore! Send the

light, _____ the bless-ed gos-pel light; let it shine _____ for-ev-er-more! 2. We have more!

Additional Lyrics

2. We have heard the Macedonian call today,
   "Send the light! Send the light!"
   And a golden off'ring at the cross we lay;
   Send the light! Send the light!

3. Let us pray that grace may ev'rywhere abound;
   "Send the light! Send the light!"
   And a Christ-like spirit ev'rywhere be found;
   Send the light! Send the light!

4. Let us now grow weary in the work of love;
   "Send the light! Send the light!"
   Let us gather jewels for a crown above;
   Send the light! Send the light!

Shall We Gather at the River?

Words and Music by Robert Lowry

Strum Pattern: 3
Pick Pattern: 3

Verse
Moderately

1. Shall we gath-er at the riv-er, where bright an-gel feet have
2. – 5. *See Additional Lyrics*

trod; _____ with its crys-tal tide for-ev-er flow-ing

Chorus

from the __ throne of __ God? Yes, we'll gath-er at the riv-er, the

beau-ti-ful, the beau-ti-ful __ riv-er. Gath-er with the saints __ at the

1. – 4.
5.

riv-er, that flows from the throne of __ God. God.

Additional Lyrics

2. On the margin of the river,
   Washing up its silver spray,
   We shall walk and worship ever
   All the happy, golden day.

3. On the bosom of the river,
   Where the Saviour King we own,
   We shall meet and sorrow never
   'Neath the glory of the throne.

4. Ere we reach the shining river,
   Lay we ev'ry burden down.
   Grace our spirits will deliver,
   And provide a robe and crown.

5. Soon we'll reach the shining river,
   Soon our pilgrimage will cease;
   Soon our happy hearts will quiver
   With the melody of peace.

Softly and Tenderly

Words and Music by Will L. Thompson

Strum Pattern: 8
Pick Pattern: 8

Additional Lyrics

2. Why should we tarry when Jesus is pleading,
   Pleading for you and for me?
   Why should we linger and heed not His mercies,
   Mercies for you and for me?

3. Time is now fleeting, the moments are passing,
   Passing from you and from me.
   Shadows are gathering, deathbeds are coming,
   Coming for you and for me.

4. Oh, for the wonderful love He has promised,
   Promised for you and for me.
   Though we have sinned, He has mercy and pardon,
   Pardon for you and for me.

The Solid Rock

Words by Edward Mote
Music by William B. Bradbury

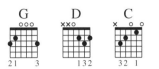

Strum Pattern: 8
Pick Pattern: 8

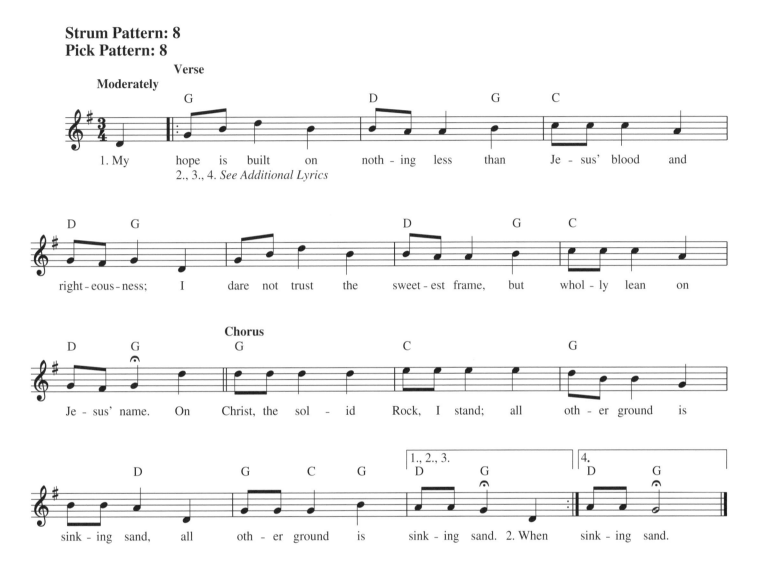

Additional Lyrics

2. When darkness veils His lovely face,
   I rest on His unchanging grace;
   In ev'ry high and stormy gale,
   My anchor hold within the veil.

3. His oath, His covenant, His blood,
   Support me in the whelming flood;
   When all around my soul gives way,
   He then is all my hope and stay.

4. When He shall come with trumpet sound,
   O may I then in Him be found;
   Dressed in His righteousness alone,
   Faultless to stand before the throne.

Spirit of God Descend Upon My Heart

Words by George Croly
Music by Frederick Cook Atkinson

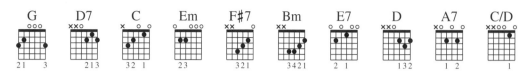

Strum Pattern: 1, 3
Pick Pattern: 2, 4

Additional Lyrics

2. Hast Thou not bid us love Thee, God and King;
   All, all Thine own: soul, heart, and strength, and mind?
   I see Thy cross, there teach my heart to cling.
   O let me seek Thee, and O let me find!

3. Teach me to feel that Thou art always nigh;
   Teach me the struggles of the soul to bear,
   To check the rising doubt, the rebel sigh;
   Teach me the patience of unanswered prayer.

4. Teach me to love Thee as Thine angels love,
   One holy passion filling all my frame;
   The baptism of the heaven-descended Dove,
   My heart an altar, and Thy love the flame.

Stand Up! Stand Up for Jesus

Words by George Duffield, Jr.
Music by George J. Webb

Strum Pattern: 3, 4
Pick Pattern: 1, 3

Additional Lyrics

2. Stand up, stand up for Jesus,
   The strife will not be long.
   This day the noise of battle,
   The next, the victor's song.
   To him that overcometh,
   A crown of life shall be.
   He with the King of glory
   Shall reign eternally.

Standing on the Promises

Words and Music by R. Kelso Carter

Strum Pattern: 3
Pick Pattern: 3

Verse
Moderately

1. Stand-ing on the prom-is-es of Christ my King. Through e-ter-nal a-ges let His
2., 3., 4. *See Additional Lyrics*

prais-es ring. Glo-ry in the high-est, I will shout and sing,

Chorus

stand-ing on the prom-is-es of God. Stand-ing, stand-ing,

stand-ing on the prom-is-es of God my Sav-ior. Stand-ing,

stand-ing, I'm stand-ing on the prom-is-es of God. God.

Additional Lyrics

2. Standing on the promises that cannot fail,
When the howling storms of doubt and fear assail.
By the living word of God I shall prevail,
Standing on the promises of God.

3. Standing on the promises of Christ the Lord,
Bound to Him eternally by love's strong cord.
Overcoming daily with the Spirit's sword,
Standing on the promises of God.

4. Standing on the promises I cannot fall,
Listening ev'ry moment to the Spirit's call.
Resting in my Savior as my all in all,
Standing on the promises of God.

Sunshine in My Soul

Words by Eliza E. Hewitt
Music by John R. Sweney

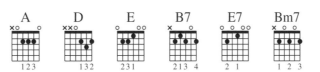

Strum Pattern: 2
Pick Pattern: 2, 5

1. There is sun-shine in my soul to-day, more glo-ri-ous and bright than glows in an-y earth-ly sky, for Je-sus is my light. O there's sun-shine, bless-ed sun-shine, when the peace-ful, hap-py mo-ments roll. When Je-sus shows His smil-ing face, there is sun-shine in my soul. 2. There is soul.

2., 3., 4. *See Additional Lyrics*

Additional Lyrics

2. There is music in my soul today,
   A carol to my King;
   And Jesus, listening, can hear
   The songs I cannot sing.

3. There is music in my soul today,
   For when my Lord is near,
   The dove of peace sings in my heart,
   The flow'rs of grace appear.

4. There is gladness in my soul today,
   And hope and praise and love,
   For blessings which He gives me now,
   For joys laid up above.

Sweet Hour of Prayer

Words by William W. Walford
Music by William B. Bradbury

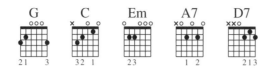

Strum Pattern: 8
Pick Pattern: 8

Additional Lyrics

2. Sweet hour of prayer,
   Sweet hour of prayer,
   Thy wings shall my petition bear;
   To Him whose truth and faithfulness
   Engage the waiting soul to bless.
   And since He bids me seek His face,
   Believe His word, and trust His grace,
   I'll cast on Him my ev'ry care,
   And wait for thee, sweet hour of prayer.

3. Sweet hour of prayer,
   Sweet hour of prayer,
   May I thy consolation share;
   Till from Mount Pisgah's lofty height
   I view my home and take my flight.
   This robe of flesh I'll drop and rise
   To seize the everlasting prize,
   And should while passing through the air,
   Farewell, farewell, sweet hour of prayer.

There Is a Balm in Gilead

African-American Spiritual

*Strum Pattern: 3, 4
*Pick Pattern: 3, 6

*Use Pattern 10 for 2/4 meas.

Additional Lyrics

2. Don't ever feel discouraged,
   For Jesus is your friend,
   Who, if you ask for knowledge,
   Will never fail to lend.

3. If you cannot preach like Peter,
   If you cannot pray like Paul,
   You can tell the love of Jesus,
   Who died to save us all.

There Is a Fountain

Words by William Cowper
Traditional American Melody Arranged by Lowell Mason

Strum Pattern: 2
Pick Pattern: 4

Verse
Moderately

1. There is a foun-tain filled with blood drawn from Im-man-uel's veins; and
2. – 5. *See Additional Lyrics*

sin-ners, plunged be-neath that flood, lose all their guilt-y stains, lose

all their guilt-y stains, lose all their guil-ty stains. And

sin-ners, plunged be-neath that flood, lose all their guilt-y stains. 2. The grave.

Additional Lyrics

2. The dying theif rejoiced to see
That fountain in his day;
And there may I, though vile as he,
Wash all my sins away,
Wash all my sins away,
Wash all my sins away.
And there may I, though vile as he,
Wash all my sins away.

3. Dear dying Lamb, Thy precious blood
Shall never lose its power,
Till all the ransomed Church of God
Be saved, to sin no more,
Be saved, to sin no more,
Be saved, to sin no more.
Till all the ransomed Church of God
Be saved, to sin no more.

4. E'er since by faith, I saw the stream
Thy flowing wounds supply,
Redeeming love has been my theme,
And shall be till I die,
And shall be till I die,
And shall be till I die.
Redeeming love has been my theme,
And shall be till I die.

5. Then in a nobler, sweeter song,
I'll sing Thy power to save,
When this poor lisping, stamm'ring tongue
Lies silent in the grave,
Lies silent in the grave,
Lies silent in the grave.
When this poor lisping, stamm'ring tongue
Lies silent in the grave.

There Is Power in the Blood

Words and Music by Lewis E. Jones

Strum Pattern: 2
Pick Pattern: 4

Verse
Moderately Fast

1. Would you be free from your bur-den of sin? There's pow'r in the blood,
2., 3., 4. *See Additional Lyrics*

pow'r in the blood. Would you o'er e-vil a vic-to-ry win? There's

Chorus

won-der-ful pow'r in the blood. There is pow'r, pow'r, won-der-work-ing pow'r in the

blood of the Lamb. There is pow'r, pow'r, won-der-work-ing pow'r in the

pre-cious blood of the Lamb. Lamb, in the pre-cious blood of the Lamb.

Additional Lyrics

2. Would you be free from your passion and pride?
   There's pow'r in the blood, pow'r in the blood.
   Come for a cleansing to Calvary's tide.
   There's wonderful pow'r in the blood.

3. Would you be whiter, much whiter than snow?
   There's pow'r in the blood, pow'r in the blood.
   Sin stains are lost in its life-giving flow.
   There's wonderful pow'r in the blood.

4. Would you do service for Jesus, your King?
   There's pow'r in the blood, pow'r in the blood.
   Would you live daily His praises to sing?
   There's wonderful pow'r in the blood.

There Shall Be Showers of Blessing

Words by Daniel W. Whittle
Music by James McGranahan

C   G7   F   Am   D7   G

Strum Pattern: 8
Pick Pattern: 8

Verse
Moderately

C   G7   C   G7   C

1. There shall be show-ers of bless-ing: This is the prom-ise of love.
2., 3., 4. *See Additional Lyrics*

F   C   Am   D7   G   G7

There shall be sea-sons re-fresh-ing, sent from the Sav-ior a-bove.

Chorus

C   G

Show - ers of bless - ing, show - ers of bless-ing we need.
(Show - ers, show - ers of bless - ing.)

C   F   C   G7   1., 2., 3.   4.
                                                 C   C

Mer-cy-drops round us are fall - ing, but for the show-ers we plead. plead.

Additional Lyrics

2. There shall be showers of blessing;
   Precious reviving rain;
   Over the hills and the valleys,
   Sound of abundance of rain.

3. There shall be showers of blessing;
   Send them upon us, O Lord.
   Grant to us now a refreshing,
   Come and now honor Your Word.

4. There shall be showers of blessing;
   O that today they might fall,
   Now as to God we're confessing,
   Now as on Jesus we call.

This Is My Father's World

Words by Maltbie Babcock
Music by Franklin L. Sheppard

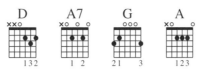

Strum Pattern: 2
Pick Pattern: 2

Additional Lyrics

2. This is my Father's world, the birds their carols raise.
The morning light, the lily white, declare their maker's praise.
This is my Father's world, He shines in all that's fair.
In the rustling grass I hear Him pass, He speaks to me everywhere.

3. This is my Father's world, oh let me ne'er forget
That though the wrong seems oft so strong, God is the Ruler yet.
This is my Father's world, the battle is not done.
Jesus who died shall be satisfied, and earth and heav'n be one.

There's a Wideness in God's Mercy

Words by Frederick William Faber
Music by Lizzie S. Tourjee

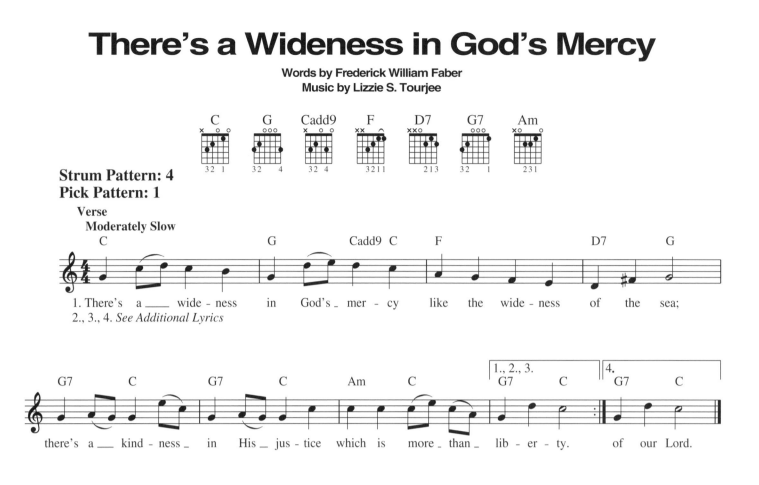

Strum Pattern: 4
Pick Pattern: 1

Verse
Moderately Slow

1. There's a ___ wide-ness in God's ___ mer - cy like the wide-ness of the sea;
2., 3., 4. *See Additional Lyrics*

there's a ___ kind-ness ___ in His ___ jus-tice which is more than ___ lib-er-ty. of our Lord.

Additional Lyrics

2. There is welcome for the sinner
   And more graces for the good;
   There is mercy with the Savior;
   There is healing in His blood.

3. For the love of God is broader
   Than the measure of man's mind;
   And the heart of the Eternal
   Is most wonderfully kind.

4. If our love were but more simple,
   We should take Him at His word;
   And our lives would be illumined
   By the presence of our Lord.

Wonderful Grace of Jesus

Traditional

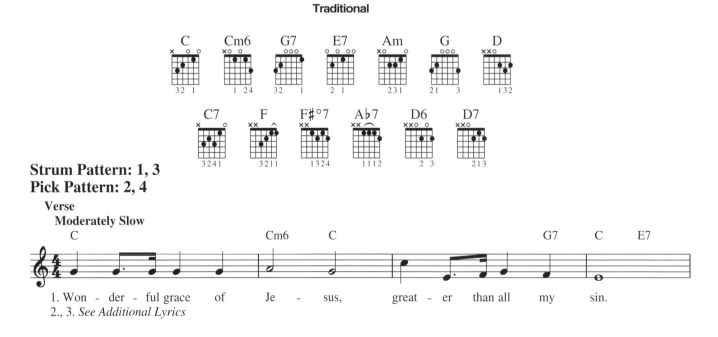

Strum Pattern: 1, 3
Pick Pattern: 2, 4

Verse
Moderately Slow

1. Won - der - ful grace of Je - sus, great - er than all my sin.
2., 3. *See Additional Lyrics*

Additional Lyrics

2. Wonderful grace of Jesus, reaching to all the lost.
   By it I have been pardoned, saved to the uttermost.
   Chains have been torn asunder, giving me liberty;
   For the wonderful grace of Jesus reaches me.

3. Wonderful grace of Jesus, reaching the most defiled.
   By its transforming power making Him God's dear child.
   Purchasing peace and heaven for all eternity;
   For the wonderful grace of Jesus reaches me.

'Tis So Sweet to Trust in Jesus

Words by Louisa M.R. Stead
Music by William J. Kirkpatrick

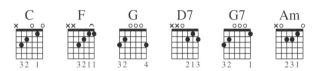

Strum Pattern: 1, 3
Pick Pattern: 2, 4

Additional Lyrics

2. O how sweet to trust in Jesus,
   Just to trust His cleansing blood,
   Just in simple faith to plunge me
   'Neath the healing, cleansing flood!

3. Yes, 'tis sweet to trust in Jesus,
   Just from sin and self to cease,
   Just from Jesus simply taking
   Life and rest and joy and peace.

4. I'm so glad I learned to trust Him,
   Precious Jesus, Savior, Friend;
   And I know that He is with me;
   Will be with me to the end.

To God Be the Glory

Words by Fanny J. Crosby
Music by William H. Doane

Additional Lyrics

2. O perfect redemption, the purchase of blood,
   To ev'ry believer the promise of God;
   The vilest offender who truly believes,
   That moment from Jesus a pardon receives.

3. Great things He hath taught us, great things He hath done,
   And great our rejoicing through Jesus the Son;
   But purer, and higher, and greater will be
   Our wonder, our transport, when Jesus we see.

We Gather Together

Netherlands Folk Hymn

Strum Pattern: 9
Pick Pattern: 7

Verse

Moderately

1. We gath - er to - geth - er to ask the Lord's bless - ing; He

2., 3. *See Additional Lyrics*

chas - tens and has - tens His will to make known. The wick - ed op -

press - ing now cease ____ from dis - tress - ing. Sing prais - es to His

name; ____ He for - gets not ____ His own. 2. Be - free!

Additional Lyrics

2. Beside us to guide us, our God with us joining,
   Ordaining, maintaining His kingdom divine.
   So from the beginning the fight we were winning.
   Thou, Lord, wast at our side; all glory be Thine!

3. We all do extol Thee, Thou Leader triumphant,
   And pray that Thou still our Defender wilt be.
   Let thy congregation escape tribulation.
   Thy name be ever praised! O Lord, make us free!

We're Marching to Zion

Words by Isaac Watts
Music by Robert Lowry

G   D7   C   Am

Strum Pattern: 8
Pick Pattern: 8

Verse
Moderately

G   D7   G

1. Come, we that love ___ the Lord, and let our joys ___ be
2., 3., 4. *See Additional Lyrics*

D7   G   C   D7   Am   D7

known; ___ join in a song with sweet ac-cord, join in a song with sweet ac-cord, and

thus sur-round the throne, and thus sur-round the throne. ___ We're

Chorus

G   D7

march-ing to Zi - on, beau-ti-ful, beau-ti-ful Zi - on. We're

G   C   G   D7 | 1., 2., 3. | 4.
                                                  G   G

march-ing up-ward to Zi - on, ___ the beau-ti-ful cit-y of God. ___ 2. Let God.

Additional Lyrics

2. Let those refuse to sing
   Who never knew our God;
   But children of the heav'nly King,
   But children of the heav'nly King,
   May speak there joys abroad,
   May speak there joys abroad.

3. The hill of Zion yields,
   A thousand sacred sweets,
   Before we reach the heav'nly fields,
   Before we reach the heav'nly fields,
   Or walk the golden streets,
   Or walk the golden streets.

4. Then let our song abound,
   And ev'ry tear be dry;
   We're marching through Immanuel's ground,
   We're marching through Immanuel's ground,
   To fairer worlds on high,
   To fairer worlds on high.

We've a Story to Tell the Nation

Traditional

Strum Pattern: 1, 3
Pick Pattern: 2, 4

Verse

Moderately

1. We've a sto - ry to tell to the na - tions that shall turn their hearts to the
2., 3., 4. *See Additional Lyrics*

right, a sto - ry of truth and mer - cy, a sto - ry of peace and

light, a sto - ry of peace and light. For the dark - ness shall turn to

dawn - ing, and the dawn - ing to noon - day bright, and Christ's great King - dom shall

come on earth; the king - dom of love and light. 2. We've a light.

Additional Lyrics

2. We've a song to be sung to the nations
   That shall lift their hearts to the Lord,
   A song that shall conquer evil
   And shatter the spear and sword,
   And shatter the spear and sword.

3. We've a message to give to the nations;
   That the Lord who reigneth above
   Hath sent us His Son to save us
   And show us that God is love,
   And show us that God is love.

4. We've a Savior to show to the nations
   Who the path of sorrow hath trod,
   That all of the world's great peoples
   Might come to the truth of God,
   Might come to the truth of God.

Were You There?

African-American Spiritual
Harmony by Charles Winfred Douglas

Strum Pattern: 3
Pick Pattern: 3

Verse

Moderately

1. Were you there when they cru-ci-fied my Lord? (Were you
2. – 5. *See Additional Lyrics*

there?) Were you there when they cru-ci-fied my Lord _____ Oh, _____

some-times it caus-es me to trem-ble, trem-ble, trem-ble. Were you there when they

cru-ci-fied my Lord? (Were you there?) 2. Were you tomb? (In the tomb?)

Additional Lyrics

2. Were you there when they nailed Him to the tree? (To the tree?)
   Were you there when they nailed Him to the tree?
   Oh, sometimes it causes me to tremble, tremble, tremble.
   Were you there when they nailed him to the tree? (To the tree?)

3. Were you there when they pierced Him in the side? (In the side?)
   Were you there when they pierced Him in the side?
   Oh, sometimes it causes me to tremble, tremble, tremble.
   Were you there when they pierced Him in the side? (In the side?)

4. Were you there when the sun refused to shine? (Were you there?)
   Were you there when the sun refused to shine?
   Oh, sometimes it causes me to tremble, tremble, tremble.
   Were you there when the sun refused to shine? (Were you there?)

5. Were you there when they laid Him in the tomb? (In the tomb?)
   Were you there when they laid Him in the tomb?
   Oh, sometimes it causes me to tremble, tremble, tremble.
   Were you there when they laid Him in the tomb? (In the tomb?)

What a Friend We Have in Jesus

Words by Joseph Scriven
Music by Charles C. Converse

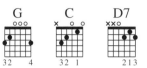

Strum Pattern: 6
Pick Pattern: 4

Verse
Moderately

1. What a friend we have in Je - sus, all our sins and griefs to bear.
2., 3. *See Additional Lyrics*

What a priv - i - lege to car - ry ev - 'ry-thing to God in prayer.

Oh, what peace we of - ten for - feit, oh, what need-less pain we bear.

All be-cause we do not car - ry ev - 'ry-thing to God in prayer. there.

Additional Lyrics

2. Have we trials and temptations,
   Is there trouble anywhere?
   We should never be discouraged;
   Take it to the Lord in prayer.
   Can we find a friend so faithful
   Who will all our sorrows share?
   Jesus knows our ev'ry weakness;
   Take it to the Lord in prayer.

3. Are we weak and heavy laden,
   Cumbered with a load of care?
   Precious Savior still our refuge;
   Take it to the Lord in prayer.
   Do thy friends despise, forsake thee?
   Take it to the Lord in prayer.
   In His arms He'll take and shield thee;
   Thou will find a solace there.

When I Survey the Wondrous Cross

Words by Lowell Mason
Music by Isaac Watts

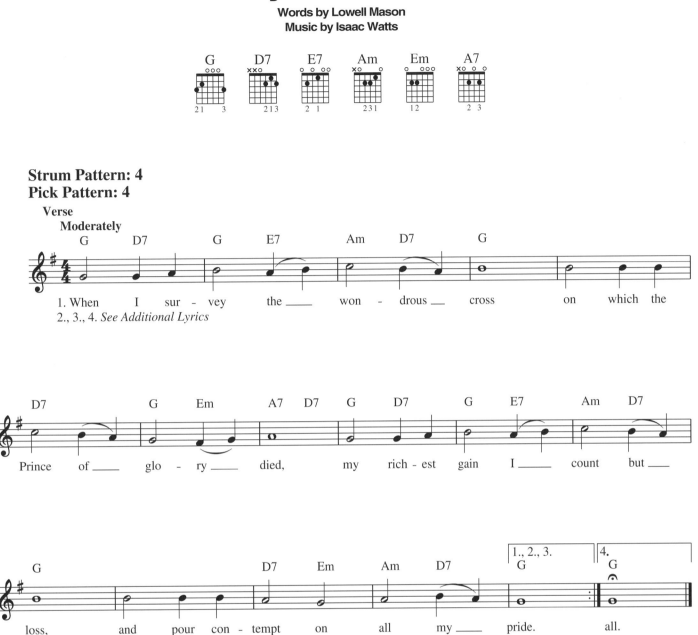

Strum Pattern: 4
Pick Pattern: 4

1. When I sur-vey the won-drous cross on which the
2., 3., 4. *See Additional Lyrics*

Prince of glo-ry died, my rich-est gain I count but

loss, and pour con-tempt on all my pride. all.

Additional Lyrics

2. Forbid it, Lord, that I should boast,
   Save in the death of Christ, my Lord.
   All the vain things that charm me most,
   I sacrifice them to His blood.

3. See, from His head, His hands, His feet,
   Sorrow and love flow mingled down.
   Did e'er such love and sorrow meet
   Or thorns compose so rich a crown?

4. Were the whole realm of nature mine,
   That were a present far too small.
   Love so amazing, so divine,
   Demands my soul, my life, my all.

When Morning Gilds the Skies

Third Verse Text by Robert S. Bridges
Music by Joseph Barnby

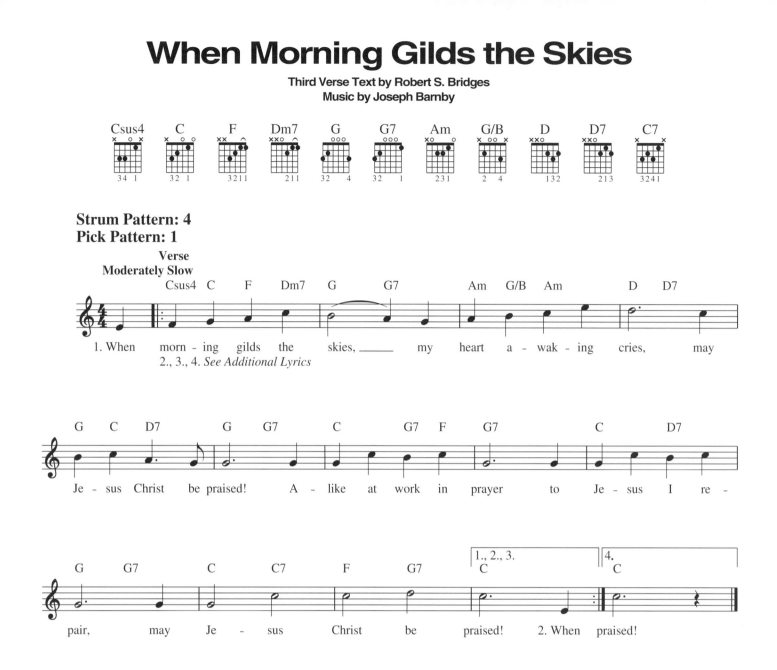

Strum Pattern: 4
Pick Pattern: 1

Additional Lyrics

2. The night becomes as day,
   When from the heart we say,
   May Jesus Christ be praised!
   The pow'rs of darkness fear
   When this sweet chan they hear.
   May Jesus Christ be praised!

3. Ye nations of mankind,
   In this your concord
   May Jesus Christ be praised!
   Let all the earth around
   Ring joyous with the sound,
   May Jesus Christ be praised!

4. Be this, while life is mine,
   My canticle divine,
   May Jesus Christ be praised!
   Be this th'eternal song
   Thro' all the ages long
   May Jesus Christ be praised!

When the Roll Is Called Up Yonder

Words and Music by James M. Black

Strum Pattern: 4
Pick Pattern: 6

Additional Lyrics

2. On that bright and cloudless morning
   When the dead in Christ shall rise,
   And the glory of His resurrection share;
   When His chosen ones shall gather
   To their home beyond the skies
   And the roll is called up yonder, I'll be there!

3. Let us labor for the Master
   From the dawn till setting sun,
   Let us talk of all His wondrous love and care;
   Then when all of life is over
   And our work on earth is done
   And the roll is called up yonder, I'll be there!

When We All Get to Heaven

Words and Music by E.E. Hewitt and J.G. Wilson

Strum Pattern: 2, 3
Pick Pattern: 3, 4

Verse
Moderately

1. Sing the won-drous love _ of __ Je - sus, sing His mer - cy _ and His grace.
2., 3., 4. *See Additional Lyrics*

In the man - sions, bright and bless - ed, He'll pre - pare for us a place. When we

Chorus

all get to heav - en, what a day of re-joic - ing that will be! When we

all see Je - sus, we'll sing and shout the vic - to - ry. ry.

Additional Lyrics

2. While we walk the pilgrim pathway,
   Clouds will overspread the sky;
   But when trav'ling days are over,
   Not a shadow, not a sigh!

3. Let us then be true and faithful,
   Trusting, serving ev'ryday.
   Just one glimpse of Him in glory
   Will the toils of life repay.

4. Onward to the prize before us!
   Soon His beauty we'll behold.
   Soon the pearly gates will open,
   We shall tread the streets of gold.

Whiter Than Snow

Words by James Nicholson
Music by William G. Fischer

Strum Pattern: 8
Pick Pattern: 8

Additional Lyrics

2. Lord Jesus, look down from Thy throne in the skies,
And help me to make a complete sacrifice;
I give up myself, and whatever I know.
Now wash me and I shall be whiter than snow.

3. Lord Jesus, for this I most humbly entreat,
I wait, blessed Lord, at Thy crucified feet;
By faith, for my cleansing I see Thy blood flow,
Now wash me and I shall be whiter than snow.

4. Lord Jesus, Thou seest I patiently wait,
Come now, and within me a new heart create;
To those who have sought Thee, Thou never saidst, "No."
Now wash me and I shall be whiter than snow.

Wondrous Love

Southern American Folk Hymn

Strum Pattern: 4
Pick Pattern: 6

Additional Lyrics

2. What wondrous love is this, oh my soul, oh my soul.
   What wondrous love is this, oh my soul!
   What wondrous love is this that caused the Lord of life
   To lay aside His crown for my soul, for my soul,
   To lay aside His crown for my soul!

3. To God and to the Lamb I will sing, I will sing,
   To God and to the Lamb I will sing.
   To God and to the Lamb who is the great I AM.
   While millions join the theme I will sing, I will sing,
   While millions join the theme I will sing.

4. And when from death I'm free, I'll sing on, I'll sing on.
   And when from death I'm free, I'll sing on.
   And when from death I'm free, I'll sing and joyful be,
   And through eternity I'll sing on, I'll sing on,
   And through eternity I'll sing on.